A Layman's Guide to
THE POET
HOMER

A Layman's Guide to THE POET HOMER

by
MAUREEN CARTER

EFSTATHIADIS GROUP

EFSTATHIADIS GROUP S.A.
14, Valtetsiou Str.
106 80 Athens
Tel: (01) 5254650, 6450113
Fax: (01) 5254657
GREECE

ISBN   960 226 565 5

© **Efstathiadis Group S.A. 1998**

Printed and bound in Greece

*To my children and their children and their children's children,
for they too might gather crumbs from The Poet's table.
Grateful thanks to my daughter in law, Lena,
for her help in finding and translating information relating to
Homer's works and on the Greek tradition of epic poetry.*

List of Illustrations

Contents

Authors note:
In simplifying Homer's two great works, the problem was not what to put in, but what to leave out. Eight hundred pages have been reduced into most of this slim book. Some lines from the Iliad and the Odyssey have been translated from Greek and these have been put into italics. Perhaps the reader will go on to study a translation from the ancient Greek in its entirety. For the works of Homer glitter with the golden garments and vessels of the gods. They shine with the sparkle of bronze and are full of the wonder of a world where gods and mortals mingle.

> "This is the god-like Homer; he who, fraught
> With wisest words, to Greece high glory brought
> And most to Argives, who the god-built Troy
> Did for fair Helen's crime by force destroy.
> Grateful to him their city here has placed
> His image, and with heavenly honours graced."

Epigram on a statue of Homer erected at Argos

Part 1

Come then, sad wives of the Trojans
whose spears were bronze, their daughters brides of disaster,
let us mourn the smoke of Ilium.

Euripedes

Why was Homer?

Why was Homer? Because it was inevitable that the spoken word, in the form of hundreds, perhaps thousands, of years of oral tradition, would, in the fullness of time, become the written word. We are lucky indeed that it was a poet such as Homer who arrived at the right time and place in history.

Those born before the 1950's can remember a time without television. For evening entertainment there was the cinema, theatre, or families gathered around the radio and, for a century or more, we have all enjoyed the printed word. Before the arrival of radio and cinema in the early 1900's, people enjoyed live theatre and music, along with reading newspapers, magazines and books. Before the eighteenth century, these latter were only for the rich. In northern Europe during the 15th century AD, villagers could look forward to the arrival of the players who performed the Miracle or religious plays and in the Dark Ages, the 5th - 11th centuries AD, again in northern Europe, the wandering minstrel played an important part in every day life. For there have always been story tellers.

In Greece the Dark Ages began in 1100 BC and lasted for almost four hundred years. Prior to this, the country had been occupied by the Achaeans, who had overrun the land, chasing away the Pelasgians or pre-Greek people. According to Greek legend, these Achaeans, or Ancient Greeks, established powerful cities such as Argos, Mycenae, Tyrins, Pylos and Sparta. And, again according to myths, they went to war with Troy. A war which lasted for ten long years.

Back in the realms of history and around 1100 BC the Dorians invaded from the north and scattered the Ancient Greeks, many of whom went to live in small settlements, from Chalcidice to the Aegean islands and across to Asia Minor. And so began the Dark Ages, for the Dorians were a simple, uncultured and war like people. During their time there was no new architecture, no innovative art or fresh ideas in science and the art of writing was lost. But there were, and had always been, the story tellers. Men who travelled from village to

village, keeping alive the traditions, telling tales, in the form of poetry and song, of ancient gods and the creation myths, handing them down from generation to generation.

The ancient Greek people had always been attracted by the power of poetry. Their first poems were religious, hymns to their gods, relating their divine ancestry. This type of poetry,

A Minstrel

sung by minstrels or bards, passed down in the oral tradition, lasted until the Dorians invaded. As the Ancient Greeks fought to establish themselves in their new colonies, the many resulting wars gave birth to brave deeds. Young heroes of war were admired by the common people, to be honoured and remembered in a new form of poetry, the "epic". Into this poetry crept tales of the long war with Troy that had taken place, so the legends went, many years earlier.

In this epic poetry the actions of the brave heroes were related and combined with the divine tales from the earlier poetry. Over the years, as the two types of story became deeply intertwined, the gods became more human, like the heroes and the heroes more divine, like gods.

We can imagine a minstrel arriving in a small village in those dark ages. The excited people sat around, transported for a while away from their hard life where they scratched a living from a stony soil. The minstrel's song was no longer only about the gods. He also sang of half forgotten kings and great palaces, war, clashing swords, great ships, wild seas and courageous deeds. The people heard of tragedy, honour and bravery caught for ever in time, woven into poetry and celebrated in a minstrel's song.

As is the way of the spoken word, these tales, many of them about real events and people, underwent changes, little elaborations over the years until at last a glimmer of light appeared after an age of darkness. Around the 8th century BC, the Dark Ages came to an end, the art of writing was re-discovered when the Greeks adopted the Phoenician alphabet and the poet Homer was born. And this is why Homer was. This was his "raison d'etre". To become the wellspring of the written epic, the inspiration for generation after generation, even to our own time. Who was this man?

Who was Homer?

Traditionally, Homer was a blind poet. The modern consensus of opinion among scholars is that he was born around 750 BC, probably in Smyrna, now the Turkish port of Izmia, but he lived and worked on the island of Chios.

We know very little about the man himself. Perhaps the great romantic English poet, John Keats, had Homer in mind when he wrote,

> *"Where's the poet? Show him! Show him,*
> *Muses nine! that I may know him."*

Homer and his works have been perused over the centuries, the study producing nothing but disagreement about him. Pausanias, the Greek traveller and writer of the 1st century BC, applied himself to the study of the bard but found the differences of opinion so great, even in his time, as to where Homer was born, what he wrote, where he died and what he was like, that he gave up. The following rhyming couplet gives us some idea of the confusion over his birthplace:

> *"Seven cities vied for Homer's birth, with emulation pious.*
> *Salamis, Camos, Colophon, Rhodes, Argos, Athens, Chios."*

Giving an example in his writings, Pausanias says that the people of Ios point out Homer's tomb and say that Klymene, buried elsewhere on the island, was his mother. But the Cypriots also lay claim to the poet, he writes, saying Themisto gave birth to him. Some said that the god Apollo was his father. One legend has it that his father was the river Melis and as a result Homer was sometimes called Melisigenis, meaning 'born from Melis'. Others say that he was fathered by the king, Meon, so was called Meonidis, meaning 'from Meon'. As to where he was buried, well, the following says it all:

*"Seven Grecian cities vied for Homer dead,
Through which the living Homer begged his bread."*

However we do know that on the island of Chios, after the death of the poet, lived the Homeridae, those who claimed to be his descendants and who travelled Greece, singing his works. These were followed by the Rhapsodes, who recited the poems holding a *rhabdos*, or small stick, as a badge of office.

Pausanias talks about Homer being cursed by a jealous heaven, losing his eyes and doomed to wander the earth as a result of great poverty. Possibly Homer was born blind, perhaps he was never blind. It could be that he lost his sight in later years. The controversy rages.

"So thou wast blind" wrote John Keats, *"...but then the veil was rent, For Jove uncurtain'd Heaven to let thee live".*

Most certainly, he was one of the greatest poets and bards, perhaps the greatest, ever to have lived. Again

A Rhapsode

there is much scholarly dispute, but it seems likely that Homer collected those wonderful and ancient oral tales from his fellow minstrels, added them to his own and wove them into the gloriously rich fabric of his two epic poems, the *Iliad* and the *Odyssey*.

These two works became central to Greek education, for Homer had provided the Greek people with heroic ideals by which to live. He had given form to their gods. Those shadowy, misty figures of the immortals took shape, solidified and were endowed for all time with human characteristics. So although they lived on ambrosia and nectar and ichor ran in their veins instead of blood, through Homer the people discovered that their gods could be deceitful and cunning, passionate and loving, tragic and comical, suffer pain and feel joy in the same way that they did.

Gods have human feelings

The gods of Homer were believed in and worshipped by the Greeks until Plato, in his *Republic*, declared that Homer's poetry should be banned for telling lies and Xenophanes, an early 5th century poet/philosopher, said that Homer had attributed to the gods "...everything that among men is a shame and a disgrace." Xenophanes visualized a single and more supernatural type of god, "..not like mortals either in body or mind". From that time people began to doubt the existence of the gods and one of the charges brought against Socrates was that he did not recognise the gods of his city. Not everyone agreed with Xenophanes but the seed of doubt had been planted. The people compromised. The gods existed, but in a more perfect form than the merry, teasing gods of Homer. Meanwhile, at last, Homer's lyrical tales could be written down. However, it is unlikely that The Poet, as he was called, could write, although possible that he dictated his works to scribes. Some say they were never written down in Homer's time, existing only in the form of traditional minstrel's songs, sung by the Homeridae and the Rhapsodes at festivals and gatherings for two hundred years. They say that only when Peisistratus came to rule Athens, circa 560 BC and became a great patron of the arts, did he order the many fragments of Homer's lyrics to be collected and written down for posterity.
Hipparchus, son of Peisistratus and a great supporter of the arts himself, introduced the recitation of Homer's entire *Iliad* and *Odyssey* at the Great Panathanaic Festival which was held, every five years and over five days, in honour of the goddess Athena. In the time of Alexander the Great, over two hundred years later, both the *Iliad* and the *Odyssey* were divided into 24 "rhapsodies", the title of each one beginning with a different letter of the Greek alphabet, from Alpha to Omega.
Herodotus, the 5th century historian, said that Homer (and

Hesiod, who came after Homer) had "given the gods their epithets, divided out offices and functions between them and described their appearance". And from this time, the Classical Age of Greece, the poet's work was read, understood, learned by heart and discussed by school boys (there were no educational establishments for girls) from the age of seven upwards. Great scholars studied his epic poems and down the centuries the works of Homer have inspired artists and poets and even generals alike.

Almost 3,000 years after he was born, Homer's two great epic poems, translated into modern Greek, are still studied by Greek school children.

The *Iliad* deals with a few days during the Trojan War, when a quarrel took place between the great warrior hero, Achilles, Admiral of the Greek fleet, and Agamemnon, King of Mycenae and commander of the Greek army.

The *Odyssey* tells of Odysseus' journey home by sea to Ithaca, from Ilium, or Troy as it is better known, at the end of the ten year long war.

The Trojan War and the characters from Homer have long been regarded as belonging in the realm of myth. But a certain German banker, Heinrich Schliemann, grew up with a passion for Homer. He believed in Troy and Agamemnon, Achilles and Odysseus. When he had made his fortune, he set out, in his retirement, circa 1874, to prove their existence. At the time there were two schools of thought concerning the whereabouts of Troy, if it had ever been. One site was on a hill near a Turkish village called Pinarbasi, and another a few miles further away, on a mound, Hissarlik. Schliemann dug at Hissarlik and uncovered what he believed to be the city of Troy, or Ilium. He found a richness of treasure, cauldrons, vases of silver, copper shields and golden cups. Priam's treasure and Helen's jewellery. Or so he thought. Unfortunately, he was an amateur archaeologist and in digging he destroyed much of the history of the many later settlements which had stood in that place. He had gone deeper than Homer's Troy and the hoard he had found belonged to a city which existed in 2,000 BC.[1] He had, though, dug up Mycenaean pottery which he later realised came from the Troy he was seeking and after his death, work continued on the site. The various settlements were numbered and it is now considered that Troy VIIa is that of Homer.

After his excavations at Hissarlik, Schliemann turned his attention to Mycenae on the Greek Peloponnese, the legendary headquarters of Agamemnon, leader of the Greek forces at Troy, according to Homer. There, the great Lions Gate had already been excavated along with some walls and Scliemann uncovered shaft graves, golden death masks, possibly one was of Agamemnon, a cup such as Homer described as belonging to Nestor and riches beyond imagination from that great civilisation, now called Mycenaean, which existed before the Dark Ages of Greece.

Through Schliemann's efforts we have come to realise that much of what Homer wrote was based on fact. The Trojan war and the great Mycenaean civilisation have entered the realms of history. We can believe the war with Troy took place around 1200 BC. Can we also believe in the great heroes, Achilles and Odysseus? Who were they?

[1] From 16th April 1996, the treasure found by Schlieman at Hissarlik goes on display for a year in the Pushkin Museum, Moscow. It has not been seen by the public for over 50 years. It was gifted to Germany by Schlieman in 1881, ordered into storage by Hitler in 1941 and found its way to Russia at the end of the World War II.

Part 2

A Simple Re-telling of The Iliad

The war with Troy, according to the ancient myth, began when Paris, son of King Priam of Troy, abducted from Greece a not unwilling Helen, wife of the Spartan King Menelaus who was brother of Agamemnon of Mycenae. (These two brothers, Agamemnon and Menelaus, were called by Homer the *Atreidae*, the sons of Atreus.) Bound by a vow, former suitors of Helen took part in the war to reclaim her. Among these were the heroes, Odysseus and Achilles and, in Homer's war, the gods also took part.

Is it ok?
For me to wear
these clothes again
~~today~~?

Who is to say?
~~that~~ I am soiled
and stinkin?
~~&~~ Unfit to display
My Self in this
way?

PHONE
Doc For
Mum

BOOK 1

When the Iliad opens, the Greeks have been camped, near their fleet and outside the walls of Troy, for nine years without matters coming to a head. Homer, in the following translation, begins with a call to the Muses, goddesses of poetry and music:

"Sing to us, Muses, of the cursed wrath of the renowned Achilles; of abundant bitternesses given to the Achaeans, great numbers of strong young men sent down to Hades, thrown to the dogs and vultures which came from all around to eat their bodies - so Zeus wanted it to happen at that time - from the moment that the two who quarrelled went their separate ways, the commander son of Atreus (Agamemnon) and the great Achilles.
Who, I wonder, among the gods, urged them to such a quarrel? The son (Apollo) of Zeus and Leto pushed them who, angry with the king, sent a plague and many of the soldiers died".

So the Iliad opens with a quarrel between Agamemnon and Achilles. During a skirmish, the Greeks had taken prisoners and one of them, a girl named Chryseis, had been seized as a prize by Agamemnon. Her father, a priest of the god Apollo, went to the king with a fortune in ransom for his daughter, but his offer was spurned. Apollo heard the priest's prayer for help and that god inflicted a terrible plague on Agamemnon's men. After the sickness had swept through the camp for ten days the leaders were assembled and Achilles suggested that the king listen to the advice of a seer. However, the wise man, Calchis, was afraid to speak out, knowing that his words would incur the royal wrath and he asked Achilles for protection. The hero promised that no harm would come to him and reluctantly, Calchis recommended that, to pacify Apollo, the king should give back the beautiful Chryseis. An angry Agamemnon insisted on some form of compensation. Achilles asked him where he thought another form of prize would come from. The king should wait until they took Troy, when he would be able to claim plunder several times the value of

the girl. Meanwhile, he should hand her back to her father.

Agamemnon agreed to send Chryseis back, but said he would claim someone else's prize in her place. Achilles rounded on the king, accusing him of profiting from war. He himself, he said, had no quarrel with Troy. He had joined

A Herald leads Briseis away

the expedition to please Agamemnon who took the pick of the spoils when he, Achilles, had done most of the fighting. When it looked as if the hero would sail for home, Agamemnon said he would take Achilles' girl, Briseis, to teach him a lesson.

At these words, Achilles drew his sword and it was only the intervention of the goddess Athena that prevented the enraged warrior from striking his monarch. She, unseen by the rest of those present, promised him gifts far greater. He had to give up Briseis and, in his anger, he refused to take any more part in the war with Troy.

The ageing Nestor got to his feet. The Trojans would be glad to hear of this quarrel, he said. Great men had listened to his advice in the past and he hoped that Agamemnon and Achilles would hear him now. The king should allow Briseis to stay with Achilles who, in turn, should be more respectful to his leader. But his words were in vain. Chriseis was taken back to her father in a ship commanded by Odysseus and Agamemnon sent his herald for Briseis. Sacrifice was made to Apollo. His praises were sung and the god, appeased, brought the plague to an end.

Achilles, having lost his girl *"of the lovely cheeks,"* sat by his ship and wept. He was heard by the goddess Thetis, his mother, who rose before him from her home in the sea. With a heart full of revenge, he begged her to ask Zeus to help the Trojans. Thetis, after telling her son that he was fated to die young, made her way to Olympus and put Achilles' request to the great god. Reluctantly, for his nagging wife, Hera, was on the side of the Greeks, Zeus agreed to the petition and Thetis departed. Zeus, that god of gods, was left to face the anger of his wife. Their quarrel was settled by Hephaestus, the smith god, son of Hera, and the happy gods made merry and drank nectar on their mountain home.

BOOK 2

Zeus had to carry out his promise. He sent Agamemnon a dream, filling him with the desire to do battle with the city of Troy at once. On waking, the king summoned his leaders, related his dream and told them to prepare the men for war. But, he announced, he was going to test his troops. He would invite them to sail for home. Then his chiefs must urge them to stay and fight.

So the men assembled, coming from their ships in droves, sitting themselves on the ground with so much noise and confusion that the heralds calling for silence could hardly be heard. Agamemnon addressed them, leaning on his staff. A staff, Homer tells us, fashioned by Hephaestus and given to Zeus, who gave it to Hermes, who presented it to Pelops, who passed it on to Atreus, who gave it to Thyestes who, on his death, left it to Agamemnon. In this way the authority with which the king spoke was conveyed.

They must leave for home in disgrace, the king announced. Nine years had gone by. Nine years of struggle to bring down the city of Troy. For nine years the forces of the Achaeans had fought a weaker enemy. Weaker, but aided by many allies. In the meantime the ships were rotting and wives and children waited at home. Agamemnon's plan almost miscarried. In spite of pleadings from his officers, the men, each filled with longing for his own hearth, rushed for their ships and the gods had to intervene to save the situation. Athena, sent by Hera, appeared to Odysseus, begging him to plead with the troops. He immediately took up the staff of Agamemnon and went among the men, urging the leaders to stand their ground and the men to wait for orders from their officers. His persuasive powers and his eloquence won the day and the great army settled down, once more assembled at the meeting place.

But one man was not happy. Thersites stood up, a lame and ugly man, often the subject of teasing by Achilles and Odysseus. He launched into a tirade against Agamemnon. Hadn't he got enough treasure? Did he need another slave girl? They should all go home and leave the king to himself with his loot.

An angry Odysseus rounded on Thersites for insulting the king and, whip in hand, struck him so hard that a great weal rose across his back. This caused

Odysseus strikes Thersites

much laughter, for Thersites was not popular. Odysseus turned to the king, saying what a pity it would be to set sail for home after waiting so long, with nothing achieved. Signs and omens had suggested that after nine years, on the tenth they would take Troy.

Nestor of Pylos rose to speak. He urged the men to stop the war of words and to remember what they had sworn to do. He appealed to the king to lead his men into the fray, sure that Zeus was on their side. Agamemnon in turn ordered the men to sharpen their weapons and attend to the horses and chariots. They were going into battle

So the men saw to their weapons and sacrificed to the gods. The heralds called them to the battle field and an invisible Athena flew through the ranks, filling each man with spirit and fire.

In a glitter of bronze, the two armies faced each other and Homer lists for us the town and cities who sent their ships and young men to the war, together with their commanders. Among them was Menestheus, who led the men from the splendid citadel of Athens. Ajax led the men from Salamis and Diomedes the men from Argos, Asine, Troezen, Tiryns of the great walls and vine clad Epidauros. Agamemnon led the forces from Mycenae, Corinth and lands around, while his brother Menelaus was in command of the men from Sparta. Nestor led the troops from Pylos and its neighbouring towns and Odysseus the proud men from Kephallonia, Zakynthos and Samos.

The Myrmidons and Hellenes stayed close to their ships, out of the fight for they had no one to command them. Their leader, Achilles, still sat and wept by the sea for his lovely Briseis.

BOOK 3

The Greeks, or Achaeans as Homer calls them, moved forward in silence while their enemy advanced with much shouting and noise. Out of the cloud of dust raised by marching Trojan feet appeared Paris, the abductor of Helen and instigator of the war. He stood alone, to challenge a Greek to single combat. On the Greek side, the wronged husband, Menelaus, stepped forward to take up the gauntlet. Paris took fright at the sight of Menelaus and retired behind his own lines, only returning after his brother, Hector *"of the flashing helmet,"* leader of the Trojan forces, taunted him, scorning him for his good looks and womanising and calling him a coward. Could Paris possibly be, he asked, the man who had sailed to foreign lands and captured the beautiful Helen? Was he afraid to face the man he had wronged? Paris admitted that his brother was right in most of the things he said but refused to be criticised for his good looks, gifts from Aphrodite. He consented to the duel with Menelaus. The winner, he suggested, would take Helen and the armies would agree a truce.

Hector stepped forward to make the announcement to both

sides and Menelaus replied, accepting the offer. Sacrifice should be made to the gods, he said, and both Priam and Agamemnon should swear the treaty.

Meanwhile, in Troy, the divine Iris, messenger of the gods, found Helen at her loom in the palace and gave her the news. Helen, weeping for Menelaus and wishing she had never left him, joined Priam, King of Troy, where he was seated with some of the elders at one of the city gates, overlooking the armies: When the king asked her who the tallest man was among the Greeks, she identified Agamemnon. He went on to ask the identity of a shorter man but broader. That, said Helen, was Odysseus. One of the elders, Antinous, spoke out. He had entertained Odysseus and Menelaus once, when they

Paris and Menelaus fight a duel

came to Troy as ambassadors. While Menelaus had been the tallest in the room and a good speaker, the seated Odysseus was more impressive. When he stood, however, he looked like a great buffoon until he spoke. Then his great voice had echoed around the hall and the power of his oratory was not to be matched. Helen named the great figure of Ajax for the king before the heralds arrived to say that it was time to make the truce. Priam had his horses harnessed to his chariot and drove with Antinous to join the Greek leaders.

Over a pair of sacrificed lambs, Agamemnon made his vow to Zeus. If Menelaus won, Helen would be his and the Trojans would pay compensation. If Paris won, Helen would stay in Troy and the Greeks depart in peace. Priam returned to his palace, for he could not bear to watch his son fight. The heralds announced the duel and lots were drawn to see who would cast the first spear. Paris won and the two put on their armour.

Watched by the opposing armies, the duel was fought and victory went to Menelaus, the goddess Aphrodite whisking Paris away before he was killed. She took him to his bedroom, where she left him before going on, in disguise, to find Helen, who had heard of Paris' downfall. While Menelaus and the Trojans searched for him, a reluctant Helen went to Paris, voicing her pleasure at his defeat. Agamemnon ordered the Trojans to give up Helen with all her riches and asked for suitable compensation for the expenses of the war.

BOOK 4

On Mount Olympus, the gods were divided in opinion. Aphrodite and Apollo were for the Trojans, Hera and Athena for the Greeks. What, Zeus asked, were they to do? Should they interfere or should they allow the truce? Hera, his wife, couldn't bear to think of Priam remaining undefeated and Zeus had made a promise to Thetis that the Trojans would have the upper hand. For a while they quarreled until they surrendered to the wishes of Zeus and Athena was dispatched to ruin the truce and to stir up the war again. So at the prompt of the goddess, who was disguised as a soldier, Pandarus the Trojan took up his great bow, fashioned from the horns of an ibex and tipped with gold, letting fly an arrow at Menelaus. It found its target, injuring the great veteran. It would have been a fatal shot, had Athena not deflected the arrow and the blood ran from a flesh wound. A horrified Agamemnon thought it was the end for Menelaus, but once reassured, he sent for the physician, Machaon, who removed the arrow and tended to the gash.

An angry Agamemnon set out to rouse his men, praising those who were eager for battle and pouring scorn on those who

Machaon tends the wounded Menelaus

were not. The Cretan King Ideomeneus promised full support and Agamemnon was thrilled to see the two Ajax brothers preparing their men. The king watched old Nestor, the great charioteer, inspiring his troops, filling them with courage and wishing he himself was young again. When Agamemnon reached Odysseus and found him idle, for he had not yet heard the call to arms, the warrior was very put out at the royal remonstration and the king had to apologise. Diomedes refused to argue with Agamemnon when he was chided for not being as brave as his father, but went straight into action. And so the battle against the forces of Troy began after all.

Homer paints us a grim picture of the struggle, with Ares, god of War, urging the Trojans and Athena, his female counterpart, driving the Greeks. With the meeting of the two armies we hear the clash of shield against shield, the splintering of bone giving way to spear and see an earth drowning in blood. Trojans and Greeks fall and all the while, Achilles, out of the battle, broods by his ships.

BOOK 5

When Diomedes, for the Greeks, slew one of the two sons of Dares, a wealthy Trojan, and the other was only saved by Hephaestus, Athena begged Ares to stop interfering and the gods retired from the battle temporarily. The Trojan army was in disarray and the Greeks filled with new heart. Agamemnon threw a Trojan leader from his chariot before spearing him to death and Menelaus killed a great hunter with a thrust from his lance. Meriones put to death the carpenter who had built the ships in which Paris had sailed to Greece and while bodies fell everywhere, Diomedes was all over the battlefield until Pandarus wounded him with an arrow in the shoulder.

Undaunted, the hero had it pulled out by Sthenelus and, at the sight of the blood which poured from the wound, Diomedes prayed to Athena for strength to kill Pandarus. That goddess appeared before him, saying,

"Fight the Trojans now, Diomedes, without fear.
I have instilled the bravery of your intrepid father Tydeus,
that owner of many horses, into your breast.
And I have lifted the mist from you eyes that you may see

the gods and know them apart from humans.
So that, if any of the immortals come to test you,
you will not harm them. Only if Aphrodite,
the daughter of Zeus, enters the battle,
then throw your sharp bronze at her."

Nothing could stop Diomedes then. One by one, young and valiant Trojans fell before his spear thrusts, leaving grieving fathers and estates with no heirs, Homer tells us. When a Trojan chief, Aeneias, saw the damage done to his men, he called upon Pandarus, saying,

"Pandarus, where are your bow, your winged arrows
and your fame? Who can be found here to compete with you?
In Lycia who, I wonder, is better than you?
Raise your arms in prayer to Zeus, then and get up
and let fly at that man over there, whoever he is."

Diomedes is chased by Pandarus

Pandarus found it hard to believe that Diomedes still lived and realised that his enemy was protected by a powerful god. He announced that his arrows were of no use, for he had pierced the armour of both Menelaus and Diomedes yet they had returned to battle stronger than ever. He bemoaned the fact that he had no chariot. In the end, he mounted the chariot of Aeneias and they drove off together after Diomedes. But they were seen by Sthenelus, who warned Diomedes and suggested that he flee. Diomedes stood his ground, saying that if he managed to kill both occupants of the chariot, then Sthenelus was to capture the horses. They would be a fine prize, for they had been bred from the mares given by Zeus in exchange for the boy Ganymede, now cup bearer on Olympus to the great god.

The spear of Diomedes, we are told in graphic detail, pierced Pandarus' nose, cut off his tongue at the root and emerged under his chin. Aeneias was saved by Aphrodite and she, while taking him from the field of battle, was chased by Diomedes. He wounded her with his spear and ordered her away. The gods came to the aid of their sister. Iris led her from the battleground. Ares drove her in his chariot to Olympus, where her mother, Dione, comforted her and healed her wound.

Sthenelus, meanwhile, remembered his orders and seized the noble horses, giving them into the care of a friend before rejoining the battlefield where Diomedes was still wreaking havoc and the gods were involved again on both sides. Three times Diomedes charged at Aeneias but Apollo removed him, taking him to his temple at Pergamus. When Ares joined the fight he roused the Trojans once more and Hector was stung into action. Aeneias, healed by the gods, took his place once more on the field. The Trojan Sarpedon was removed from the fray and a spear removed from his thigh. Hector was accompanied and protected in the battle by Ares and the Greeks began to fall back. At this, Athena and Hebe made their way to Olympus, where Zeus gave Athena permission to deal with the War god. So the Goddess donned her armour and visited the battle ground where she found an exhausted Diomedes. What was the matter with him, she wanted to know. Was he frightened? The warrior reminded her that she had told him not to fight the immortals, except for Aphrodite, and it was Ares who was his problem. Athena allowed him to wound another immortal. Ares, called the Butcher by Homer, was speared in the belly, whereupon he flew to Olympus to be healed.

BOOK 6

The battle continued. For a while the tide turned in favour of the Greeks, or Achaeans, as Diomedes, Agamemnon, Menelaus and the ageing Nestor put new heart into the men by their daring actions. At one point, a Trojan warrior fell from his chariot when his runaway horses crashed into a tree. Menelaus caught up with him and would have spared him had not Agamemnon arrived and pointed out that the Trojans had not spared even the lives of mothers amd babies when they had occupied his home.

When it looked as if the Greeks were putting their enemies to flight, Priam's son, Helenus, begged Hector to rally his men and ask his women to sacrifice to Athena and pray to her to keep the terrible Diomedes away from Ilium (Troy). Hector took his advice, put new fire into his men and immediately the Trojans gained ground.

In a sudden space on the battlefield, Diomedes confronted a Trojan soldier and challenged him to combat. He admired him for his daring and asked his name and whether he was a mortal, before taking up his sword against him. And Homer furnishes us with a wonderful tale within a tale, as Glaucus, son of Hippolochus, related the story of his ancestry.

In a part of Argos, he said, lived Sisyphus, a cunning rascal. The son of Sisyphus was Glaucus, who was the father of Bellerophon, a handsome youth. The local king, Proetus, had a wife, Anteia, who fell in love with Bellerophon. The lad spurned her advances and the angry queen told her husband that Bellerophon had attempted rape. The king, who dared not have Bellerophon put to death, banished him, sending him, with a sealed note, to his father in law , King of Lycia. The note demanded Bellerophon's demise.

When the king of Lycia saw his son in law, he called for celebration. The feasting over, in the light of "*rosy fingered dawn,*" the king read the note proffered by Bellerophon and decided to give him a dangerous task before he put him to death. In fact, the task was so perilous that he thought it could save him the problem of killing the boy, for the lad would probably not survive the ordeal. Bellerophon was told to kill the Chimaera, a monster with a serpent's tail, a goat's body and a lion's head which breathed fire. With the aid of the gods, the lad succeeded in his task and on returning to the king, was given more terrible assignments. When the boy accomplished all the tasks and returned unharmed, the king realised that Bellerophon was watched over by the gods. He offered the boy his daughter in marriage and gave him half of his realm. The pair had three children, Isander, Hippolochus and Laodameia. Bellerophon eventually angered the gods and died in poverty and alone. Ares killed Isander and Artemis put Laodameia to death. The only surviving child was Hippolochus. Glaucus was his son.

Diomedes took great pleasure in the story, for his grandfather,

Oeneus, had once entertained Bellerophon and the two had exchanged gifts. So Diomedes and Glaucus forgot the war for a moment, clasped each other's hands and exchanged armour, Diomedes doing better in the exchange, for his armour was bronze and that of Glaucus was gold.

Meanwhile, Hector went to the palace of King Priam to urge

Hector says farewell to Andromeda

the women to pray for Trojan victory, but even though they took rich gifts to Athena's temple, that goddess would not listen. Hector made his way to the beautiful home of Paris, where the handsome youth was sitting with his fair Helen. An angry Hector rebuked Paris, for the war was his fault and he was not doing his duty. Paris asked Hector to wait while he put on his armour and Helen, admitting her guilt, wishing she had never been born, asked Hector to sit a while. Hector, though, had to be on his way, for he wished to see his wife and son, perhaps for the last time.

On the walls of Troy, Hector met his wife, Andromache, who carried their baby son in her arms. Andromache pleaded with her husband, asking him to remember that he had a duty not only to Troy, but also to his son and to her, for her father, King of Thebes, had been struck dead by Achilles at the sacking of that city. Her seven brothers were also killed by Achilles and her mother taken by him as a slave, only to die at the hands of Artemis. In tears, Andromache begged Hector not to return to the field but to rally his troops from the safety of the battlements. And Hector *"of the glittering helmet"* replied in character. He could not show his face in Troy again if he behaved in such a cowardly fashion. He told Andromache he was not afraid of the death he was sure was approaching, but of what would happen to her as a slave in the hands of the Greeks. He went to take his son in his arms but the child was terrified at the sight of his father in his plumed, shining helmet. Hector removed it, bid a tender farewell to wife and child and Paris caught up with him as he made for the battleground once more.

BOOK 7

The sight of Hector and Paris re-joining the battle put new heart into the Trojans. But as Greeks fell to the spear thrusts of Paris, Hector and Glaucus, once again the gods intervened. Athena and Apollo met and planned a delay in the fighting by way of another duel. Their scheme was put into motion and both armies sat down gladly. Athena and Apollo watched, pleased at the sight of the troops:

"sitting there, in close file, their helmets and lances swaying like the rippling and darkening of the sea when the rising West Wind rises blows suddenly."

Hector dared the Achaeans to put up their champion. His challenge was met by silence until, at last, Menelaus stood up, ashamed of his reluctant companions in arms. As he went to put on his armour, Agamemnon called him back, admiring him for his bravery but knowing that Hector was the better man by far. Even Achilles had been in awe of him. Nestor got to his feet and berated the men. When he was a youth, he recalled, and fought with troops at the river Celadon, they were challenged by a great warrior and, although Nestor was the youngest there, no one but he dared confront the man. With the help of Athena he was victorious. How he longed to be young again, for here he was, amongst the best men in the land, yet no one would stand against Hector. He was appalled at their unwillingness to accept the challenge. With that, nine men stood up, among them Agamemnon, Diomedes, the Ajax brothers and Odysseus and the Greeks had to choose one of them. They drew lots.

Ajax and Hector fight

The winner was the Greater Ajax, and even Hector quailed at the sight of that mighty man striding forward, shield glittering in the sunlight. The duel began and although Ajax was the first to draw blood and both men resorted to hurling rocks, the fight was so even that at length heralds from both sides intervened, suggesting that, as it was getting dark, the duel be brought to an end. Hector nobly called off the fight and the two exchanged gifts. In the Greek camp, Agamemnon sacrificed a bull to Zeus and a meal was made of it, Ajax being offered the choicest piece of meat.

Then wise old Nestor proposed a truce, while they removed their dead from the field of battle and made a funeral pyre. They should, said the elderly warrior, build a barrow over the pyre and from either side of it, construct a high wall around the camp and ships, with strong gates and a path by way of which the chariots could come and go. Outside the wall and parallel to it, they should dig a deep trench.

Meanwhile, in the Trojan camp trouble brewed. Antenor suggested calling an end to the war and returning Helen and her possessions to the Greeks. Paris at once objected, refusing to return his wife, but offered to return all the riches he had plundered from Argos. King Priam announced that they would go down with the offer to *the hollow ships* of the Achaeans the next morning, when they would also ask for a respite in order to bury their dead.

And so it was that, the next day, both sides agreed the truce, but Paris' offer was refused by Agamemnon. Sorrowful Greeks and Trojans alike removed their dead and burned the bodies. In the early hours of the following morning, following the advice of Nestor, the Greeks set about building the high protective wall around their camp and ships. By nightfall it was complete and the trench dug. Behind the safety of their new defences, the Greeks feasted and drank the wine which had arrived in a ship piloted by the son of that great hero, Jason. The gods had watched the activity from the heights of

Olympus. An indignant Poseidon protested that the wall had gone up without the customary sacrifices being offered to the gods. But Zeus told him not to worry. When the Greeks sailed for home, he could knock it down.

BOOK 8

High on Olympus, Zeus assembled the gods. He wished, he told them, for matters to be brought to a quick conclusion and ruled that he would punish any god who helped either Greek or Trojan. Then he drove his golden chariot to Mount Ida, from whose heights he could gaze out over Troy and the Greek ships.

On the ground outside the walls of Troy battle recommenced and was fought evenly until midday. Then Zeus weighed death for both sides in his scales. On the side for the Trojans fate weighed lightly but the balance dropped low and heavy on the other side. The fortunes of the Greeks, at least for a while, were determined and, terrified by a lightning flash from the god, they lost heart. The two mighty Ajax brothers, and Agamemnon and Odysseus all turned back towards their

*Zeus watches
from Mount Ida*

ships. Even brave Nestor would have left the field but his horse was in trouble. He was rescued by Diomedes, for Hector was taking advantage of the old man's problem. The gallant Diomedes let fly an arrow at the Trojan prince but missed and killed his charioteer. A great thunderclap from Zeus frightened the horses of Diomedes and Nestor urged him to flee, for he could see that Zeus had sided with Troy. To the jeers of Hector, Diomedes reluctantly turned his horses away and was forced into retreat by continuing thunderbolts hurled by Zeus. Hector gloated as the Greeks fell back and called on his men to go forward. Their horses could jump the trench, he said, and the wall would not hold them back. They would fire the Greek ships. The watching goddess, Hera, begged Poseidon to intervene but he refused to go against the wishes of his brother Zeus.

Agamemnon, full of contempt for his men, shamed them into battle once more and interceded with the great Zeus who was moved by his prayer. Diomedes led the men back into the fray. The great bowman, Teucer, fought beside his half brother,

Ajax. He would step out from behind the shield of the warrior, let fly an arrow and then retire behind the shield once more for safety. Many Trojans fell, pierced by his arrows, until he let fly at Hector, missed him and once more that prince lost a charioteer. An angry Hector picked up a rock and hit Teucer on the shoulder as he was putting another arrow to his bow. The string of his weapon broke and before he was injured further Ajax shielded him again and he was carried off the field.

Then Zeus swayed the battle in favour of the Trojans from his mountain viewpoint and Hera and Athena schemed to defy the great god's ruling and go to the aid of the Greeks. They armed themselves, harnessed their horses to a golden chariot and drove out through the heavenly gates. But an angry Zeus saw the pair leave and sent his messenger, Iris, to turn them back, promising dire results if they refused.

The two goddesses returned to Olympus, where Zeus told them the Greeks would suffer even more, until Achilles joined the fight. It was decreed. They could do nothing. Darkness fell, thus saving the Greeks from immediate defeat and Hector gathered his army, forecasting success for the next day, telling them to feast and make merry but to keep fires burning all night, in order to see, in case the Greeks made a dash for their ships and home.

BOOK 9

The Greeks had lost heart. A despairing Agamemnon suggested boarding the ships and sailing for home. Horrified, Diomedes stood and accused his king of lacking courage. He and Sthenelus would fight on. Wise old Nestor rose and supported him, but suggested that they post sentries and prepare a meal. Then he himself would speak to them.

Appetites appeased, Nestor got to his feet and proposed that Agamemnon make up his quarrel with Achilles and apologize to him for taking the girl, Briseis. Agamemnon knew he had committed a grave error when he quarrelled with a man who was worth a whole army. He announced that he would offer Achilles many riches as well as returning the girl to him. If they defeated the Trojans, Achilles would have a share of the spoils and on returning home, he could take one of the daughters of the king as a wife, together with a large dowry.

It was agreed that Ajax and Odysseus would take Agamemnon's offer to Achilles and the two set out, worried that the hero's pride would get the better of him and he would refuse the offer of the king. With them went the aged Phoenix, who had accompanied Achilles to Troy as guardian and companion but remained with Agamemnon and his men after the quarrel.

When they arrived at the hero's hut, they were greeted like long lost friends. Much encouraged, after they had eaten and were seated by a good fire with a goblet of wine in their hands, Odysseus began to speak. He told Achilles how bad things were for them and begged him to return to the fight, listing the gifts of the king and conveying his apology. However, he said, it was not only for those things that Odysseus should return, but for his exhausted fellow men.

Achilles was sour. No man, he said, got thanks for fighting. Those who did battle and those who stayed behind got the same share. Be you industrious or be you lazy, you died the same death. No, he would not help. He was not responsible for starting the war and if they looked out to sea the next morning, they would see his ships heading for home. He wanted neither Agamemnon's gifts nor any of his daughters. Achilles finished by suggesting they all followed his example and went home, for the greatest of gods, the almighty Zeus, was protecting Troy.

A weeping Phoenix, torn between his devotion and responsibility as guardian to remain with Achilles, and his loyalty to the Greek cause, begged him to stay and fight. How, he asked, could he himself stay on alone if Achilles left? He

*Odysseus speaks
to Achilles*

appealed to him to master his pride, reminding him that through prayer, the gods could be influenced to change their minds. He asked him not to reject the words of Odysseus and Ajax lightly. He reminded Achilles of an old story. Meleager refused to help the Aetolians when the Curetes were storming the walls of their city, Calydon. Only when the battlements had been scaled and put to fire and shots reached his house, did Meleager listen to the pleas of his wife and put on his armour. The city was saved but Meleager received none of the gifts promised to him. Phoenix begged Achilles not to wait until it was almost to late, when the ships had been fired by the Trojans, but to go to the aid of Agamemnon while the Achaeans thought well of him and the gifts were still on offer.

Achilles cared nothing for the opinions of the Achaeans, and said as much to Phoenix. "*Something else I will say to you, and keep it in mind,*" said Achilles. "*Do not move my heart any more with tears and groans.*" He would not be swayed by Phoenix, but offered him a bed for the night, saying at dawn he would decide whether to sail for home or not.

Ajax, seeing that things were hopeless, suggested to Odysseus that they might as well leave. He accused Achilles of being proud and hard-hearted and caring little for his fellow men, to be so outraged over a girl. But he wanted to part as friends.

Achilles recognized that much of what Ajax said was right, but he insisted that until his own ships and huts were put to fire by Hector, he would not enter the war. So Odysseus and Ajax left and Phoenix and Achilles prepared themselves for sleep.

Back in the camp, in the royal hut and in horrified silence, Agamemnon and his men listened as Odysseus made his report. The stillness was broken by Diomedes. Achilles, he said, would fight as and when his conscience allowed. Meanwhile, he suggested, everyone should get a good night's sleep and in the morning Agamemnon would lead his men, taking his position in the front line.

BOOK 10

Agamemnon could not sleep. He could see the Trojan fires and hear their music and merry making. Putting on a lion skin and taking up a spear, he set out in the darkness to talk with the wise old Nestor. However, he was not the only one abroad that night, for Menelaus, acutely aware that it was on his behalf that the Greeks were at war, was also restless. The two met and agreed they must hold a conference to discuss the grave situation. Menelaus set out to rouse Ajax and Agamemnon continued on his way to Nestor's tent.

Nestor, after listening to the anxious Agamemnon, was soon up and dressed and he went to wake Odysseus (who joined him willingly) and Diomedes, who did not much like being deprived of his sleep but realising the seriousness of their situation woke two more leaders in his turn. When all were met, Nestor spoke out. Someone, he said, should spy on the Trojans and discover their plans for the next day. At once Diomedes offered to go, picking Odysseus as his companion. The pair armed themselves, offered a prayer to Athena and set out for the Trojan camp.

But among the Trojans, Hector had not been able to sleep. He had gathered his council together and the outcome of the meeting was that Dolon, rich son of a herald and fleet of foot, would sneak into the Greek camp and see how well their ships were guarded. Dolon had offered to do this, asking for Achilles' horses and chariot as a reward for his services.

Dolon set out for the Greek camp and the unlucky man was soon spotted by Odysseus and Diomedes. They allowed him to pass them under cover of darkness and then gave chase. They caught the man just before he ran into the sentries guarding the Greek ships and the terrified Dolon promised them a fortune in ransom if only they let him live. He told them that Hector was in conference, that the Trojans themselves put up no special sentries, for each family kept watch for itself and

Odysseus captures Thracian horses

that their allies, some of them newcomers like the Thracians, slept without watching at all. The Thracian king, he said, posessed the most beautiful, fast, snow white horses. When Dolon had finished speaking he was killed and his body buried before Diomedes and Odysseus continued on their way, this time to the Thracian camp, where they found Rhesus, King of Thrace, sleeping with his men alongside their horses and equipment.

Diomedes put Rhesus and twelve men to death by the sword before Odysseus had the horses untied and, at the suggestion of Athena, after he had slain the Thracian king, the two rode fast for their own camp before they were caught. The god Apollo, angry that Athena was again handing out advice to the Greeks, woke a Thracian leader who saw the carnage and his cries brought the horrified Trojans to the spot.

Nestor heard the approach of galloping horses and was first to greet Odysseus and Diomedes. Thankful for their safe return he congratulated the pair and admired the beautiful white Thracian horses they had brought with them, wondering whether they were a gift from Athena or even Zeus himself. Odysseus, laughing, explained what had happened and tied the animals up outside Agamemnon's hut. Then he and Diomedes washed off the sweat of the expedition in the sea, bathed, oiled themselves and poured a libation of thanks to Athena before eating, drinking a draught of wine and going to their beds.

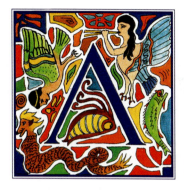

BOOK 11

As the new day broke, both sides prepared for battle once more. Agamemnon put on his bronze armour; greaves for his legs and on his upper body a cuirass or breast plate decorated in blue enamel and gold. A studded sword went into a silver sheath and the king took up his great shield of bronze, an enamel boss in the centre. On his head he wore a plumed helmet and he carried bronze headed spears.

The two armies fell upon each other and the battle was even for some hours, until the Greeks broke through the enemy lines and Agamemnon seized the advantage. Like Diomedes before him, Agamemnon was everywhere on the battlefield, doing such damage that the Trojans were put to flight and had almost reached the city walls when Zeus intervened. The goddess Iris took his message to Hector, telling him to rally his men but stay out of the fight himself until he saw Agamemnon wounded. Then the ruler of the gods would give him strength and he would push the Greeks back to their ships by nightfall.

So the Trojans turned and Agamemnon charged, killing a son of the Trojan Antenor, before the boy's brother took his revenge and struck the king with his spear, wounding him in the arm. Agamemnon fought on for as long as he could but eventually his injury forced him to retire from the fray. Hector seized his chance and put new heart into his men. Diomedes in turn rallied the Greeks and for a while the battle was even once more, but the Greeks had lost heart and most of the fighting was left to Odysseus and Diomedes. Diomedes struck Hector but only temporarily dazed him. Paris wounded Diomedes with an arrow which pierced his foot and when the great warrior had to retire from battle, it was left to Odysseus alone to fight on. He was soon surrounded by Trojans, but put many to the sword before he was struck in the side with a spear. Pulling the weapon out and seeing the blood flow, Odysseus called for help and Menelaus and Ajax came to his aid. While Ajax hurled himself at the Trojans, Menelaus got Odysseus back to his chariot and away from the battle.

Hector, meanwhile, was engaged in conflict with Nestor but, when the Greek captain and surgeon, Machaon, was wounded severely in the shoulder, Nestor took him back to the ships for attention, for his services were needed. Hector was free to go after Ajax. Outnumbered, Ajax was forced to retreat, fighting as he did so.

While Ajax was in retreat, Achilles, from his ships, was watching the progress of the battle and saw Nestor escorting a wounded man away. He sent his great friend, Patroclus, to see who was injured. On reaching Nestor's hut, Patroclus found the old soldier and Machaon quenching their thirst. Nestor, outspoken as usual, said he could not understand why Achilles should be concerned about one wounded man while disregarding the anguish of the whole army. Old Nestor told Patroclus how he longed for the vigour of youth. He related how he had fought for Pylos against the Elians. At that time his horses were hidden from him, for he was forbidden to fight on account of his youth. Disregarding the order, he had gone with the army on foot and when the two armies met, the first man fell to him, along with fifty chariots.

Achilles, said Nestor, was brave, but no one could make use of his courage. He and Odysseus, he reminded Patroclus, had been the ones to enlist him and Achilles into Agamemnon's army. As the two were given advice by their elders before leaving, Patroclus' father had said that although Achilles was stronger and more aristocratic, Patroclus was older and must set an example and give advice to the younger man. Perhaps, said Nestor, it was not too late to remember those words. But, if it was an order of the gods that stayed Achilles' hand, then at least he could give Patroclus his armour and let him fight in his place, allowing the Trojans to believe Achilles had taken up his sword against them at last.

Patroclus, on his way back to Achilles, met a wounded Greek, Eurypylus, staggering back to camp. In

*Patroclus helps
the wounded Europylus*

answer to the young man's enquiry, Eurypylus said there was little hope left, as the Trojans grew stronger, but at least Patroclus could help him, and cut the arrow from his flesh. Whereupon Patroclus took the wounded man to his tent and tended to him, removing the arrow, washing away the blood and applying herbs to the wound.

BOOK 12

The battle had reached the Greek wall which, fronted by a deep trench, surrounded their ships. This wall, built without proper sacrifice to the gods, lasted only until Troy had fallen and the Greeks were sailing for home. Then, as Zeus had suggested, Poseidon destroyed it by bringing together the rivers and streams which ran down from Mount Ida. With the help of torrential rain provided by Zeus, Poseidon guided the flood waters and demolished the defences.

But for the moment, the wall stood, with the Greeks manning its towers sorely pressed by Hector and his men. It was impossible for the Trojans to negotiate the ditch, which had been dug in front of the ramparts, in chariots. So at the suggestion of Polydamus and led by Hector, five great companies left their horses behind and attacked the wall on foot. Meanwhile, the Trojan Asius led his company of chariots to the one gate left open in the wall, approached by a causeway, which allowed the Greeks to return to their ships from battle. But the gate was held by two gallant Lapiths who defended it with rocks and stones for weapons until Asius cried out to the gods in despair. Then the Lapiths went on the attack, stabbing swords and casting spears until many Trojans lay dead around them.

Meanwhile, in spite of an ill omen, which appeared in the form of an eagle carrying a blood red snake in its claws, Hector attempted to storm the wall with his infantry. Zeus caused a fierce wind to blow dust in the face of the Greeks and the Trojans took advantage of it, attempting to pull down the towers and Greeks and Trojans alike pelted each other with rocks and stones. Sarpedon of Troy, inspired by Zeus and with the aid of Glaucus, pressed forward and Menestheus, for the Greeks, called upon Ajax and his brother, Lesser Ajax, for help. Ajax answered the call, taking his half brother, Teucer, with him. Ajax killed Sarpedon's comrade in arms and Teucer slew Glaucus. An enraged Sarpedon breached the wall but was struck by Teucer's arrow, which did not penetrate but he fell back when his shield was hit by Ajax. He called to his men for help and they rushed to his aid, but the Greeks had also called for reinforcements and once more the battle on the wall was equal. Shield clashed with shield, spear rang on spear, lance bit into flesh and the wall and ground were soaked in blood.

At last Hector, inspired by Zeus, called his men forward as he lifted a great rock and hurled it at a doorway in the wall. Leaping through the splintered wood, he was followed by his troops who swarmed through and over the fortifications and the Greeks turned to flee for their ships.

Hector hurls a great rock

BOOK 13

Zeus, happy with the way things were going and sure that no other god would intervene, left the scene. But the brother of Zeus, the great Poseidon, god of the sea, left the mountain from which he, too, had been watching the battle closely, and made his way to the Greek camp where Hector and his men were so close to capturing the enemy ships. Disguised as the seer, Calchas, the god approached Ajax and his brother, the Lesser Ajax, filling them with new hope and spirit, telling them that they could win, if only the two of them would make a stand there, at the breach in the wall, against Hector. When Poseidon left them, the brothers realised that they had been addressed by a god and were filled with eagerness for the fight. As they were talking, the god went on to encourage the rest of the Greeks who were feeling demoralised and defeated. Still in the guise of the seer, he goaded them into action with his oratory and they formed up as a solid wall in support of the two Ajax brothers and Hector and his men were confronted.

Hector encouraged his troops when they came up against the closed ranks of the Greeks and Deiphobus, his brother, stepped to the fore. Meriones hurled his spear at him but it

*Poseidon goes
to the Greek camp*

struck the Trojan's shield and broke. As Meriones retired from the fray to find a new lance, Teucer struck the Trojan, Imbrius and, as he was stripping the body of its armour, Hector aimed his spear at him but it missed and struck Amphimachus, grandson of Poseidon. Ajax hurled his spear at Hector, hitting his shield with such force that the Trojan leader had to fall back as the Greeks removed the two dead bodies.

Mourning for his grandson, Poseidon met Idomeneus, who was returning to his hut, having escorted a wounded man from the battle. The god spurred him into action and on his way back to the fight, Idomenus met Meriones, who was looking for a new spear. Together they returned, deciding, on the way, that Ajax and his brother were faring well in the centre so they would go to the aid of those fighting on the left wing. And there they fought, while Zeus, back on watch, encouraged the Trojan side. Poseidon inspired the Greeks, flitting about amongst them in disguise, for he feared the anger of his powerful brother.

With a spear throw, Idomeneus killed the man who was betrothed to Cassandra, daughter of King Priam. As he dragged the body away he was charged by Asius in a chariot, but Idomeneus slew him with another throw of his spear, which pierced his enemy's throat. Deiphobus, maddened when Idomeneus killed Asius, hurled his spear but missed Idomeneus, killing a Greek chieftain instead, bragging about his act of revenge. An enraged Idomeneus aimed his spear and killed Alcathous and, saying that he had killed three to one of Deiphobus, challenged that Trojan to a personal fight. Deiphobus appealed for help to Aeneas, brother in law of Alcathous and Idomeneus called to his own companions. And so the battle on the left wing raged fiercely, as the two, supported by their friends, clashed in anger. Priam's son, Helenus joined in for Troy and Menelaus for Greece.

Hector, in the centre of the battle ground, unaware of the events taking place on his left., faced the two Ajax brothers who fought side by side. When the Trojan leader was on the point of retreat, Polydamus encouraged him and Paris joined him. They had breached the wall, but could not break the Greek line.

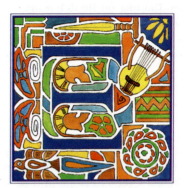

BOOK 14

Old Nestor in his hut, on hearing the noise of battle, went outside and was horrified to see that the wall had been broken. For a while the ageing warrior was uncertain what to do. Eventually he made up his mind to speak to Agamemnon and on his way he met the king returning wounded from the fight, accompanied by the bloodstained Diomedes and Odysseus. Agamemnon suggested launching the ships in readiness to flee. A shocked Odysseus scorned him for his bad leadership and Agamemnon admitted to being wrong but asked for a better plan. Diomedes suggested that, although they were wounded and could not fight, at least they could go on to the battle field and urge their men to action. And so the four were agreed.

Meanwhile, Hera, wife of Zeus, happy to see Poseidon aiding the Greeks, also saw that Zeus had returned to Ida, his mountain top viewpoint. She bathed, anointed her body with scented oils, combed out her hair and dressed herself in her most alluring clothes. She approached Aphrodite and asked for and received the powers of love and longing, which were

*Hera gets ready
to visit Zeus*

woven into a girdle. She told Aphrodite that she needed the powers to heal a long standing quarrel between two of their fellow divinities. Aphrodite willingly parted with her precious embroidered girdle and Hera went on to visit the god of Sleep, asking him to close the eyes of Zeus once she was in his arms, promising a reward of a golden chair fashioned by the smith god, Hephaestus. Sleep was reluctant. He had put Zeus to sleep once before for Hera and narrowly missed being thrown from the heavens as a result of the great god's anger. In the end he granted her wish, but only in return for one of the Graces, with whom he had fallen in love.

Hera sought out Zeus who was immediately filled with desire for her and, as he took her into his arms, he fell into a deep sleep. Poseidon was free to aid the Greeks and set out at the head of Agamemnon, Diomedes and Odysseus, his sword flashing like lightning. Homer wrote that:

> *"Neither the waves of the sea on the reefs, raised*
> *from the deep by the harsh north wind, nor the fire which*
> *suddenly inflames the mountain above,*
> *held threatening in the thickets until it reaches*
> *and roars in the trees, nor the howling of wind blowing*
> *in the high oaks, moaning in rage with all its might,"*

none of these made so much noise as the meeting of the two armies sounding their terrible war cries."

When Hector's spear missed Ajax, the latter hurled a rock at the Trojan commander, who fell and was taken from the field and laid out by the river. For a moment he was revived with the cool water but soon fell unconscious again.

Encouraged by the fall of Hector, the Greeks took heart. Soon Teucer, Meriones and Agamemnon were putting Trojans to the sword. Once more Homer describes in graphic detail the terrible wounds meted out by the spear thrusts of men on both sides though most fell to Lesser Ajax and suddenly the Trojans were in retreat.

BOOK 15

Zeus woke to see Hector lying gasping on the ground and the Trojans withdrawing. Guessing that his wife was responsible in some way, he raged at her, reminding her of the time he had hung her from the heavens, tied with a golden chain, her feet weighted with lead. Hurriedly, Hera told Zeus that she had not urged Poseidon to help the Greeks and her husband was pacified. He instructed her to go to Olympus and send Iris and Apollo to him, for he had work for them. The Greeks would fall back, he said, to their ships. Patroclus would be slain by Hector, who would, in turn, be killed by Achilles. Only then would the Greeks take Troy and, until that time, no other gods were to interfere.

An angry Hera reached Olympus where the impulsive Ares had to be held back by Athena and prevented from joining the battle on the side of the Trojans, to avenge the death of one of his sons. Iris and Apollo flew, as requested, to Zeus. Iris was dispatched to Poseidon, to instruct him to return to his kingdom under the sea. Apollo was sent to instill courage into Hector, until the Greeks were driven back to their ships. At that point, said Zeus, he would decide what to do next.

*Teucer breaks
the string
of his bow*

Poseidon reacted strongly to Iris' message from his brother. Wasn't he equal in status to Zeus, he fumed? He would not obey the order. Iris warned him that the Furies always took the side of the great god, and it was better that he did as he had been told. Poseidon recognized the wisdom of Iris' words but cautioned her that, if Zeus allowed Troy to stand, he would have nothing further to do with him.

Apollo found Hector barely conscious, but the powerful god breathed new heart into the warrior who leapt for his chariot and led his men into battle once more. At the sight of Hector, whom they had believed dead, the Greeks lost heart and all would have run had it not been for Thoas. He suggested that the best men stay and hold Hector back while the rest returned to the ships. But a valiant Thoas and his men fought not only Hector but Apollo as well. In the end it was hopeless. When Thoas was forced back behind the Greek wall, Apollo

and Hector charged, leading the Trojan chariots. The wall fell
and the Greeks fled for the ships, praying out loud to Zeus for
help. Meanwhile, Patroclus, still tending the wounded
Eurypylus, saw what was happening and decided to go to
Achilles to persuade him to fight.

As the Greeks fought to defend their ships, the battle reached
a state of stalemate. Hector and Ajax fought over one ship and
Ajax killed Hector's cousin. Hector retaliated and slew a
friend of Ajax. Teucer was called upon to use his great archery
skills but the string of his bow broke.

This encouraged Hector, who told his men that it was a sign
that Zeus was on their side. He tried to break through the
enemy line once more, but it held firm until Hector:

> *"shining all over, swooped and landed in their midst,*
> *like a wave which, nourished by the winds and the clouds,*
> *falls on a fast boat, burying it whole in its foam and the wild*
> *breath of the wind whistles high in the rigging*
> *and the sailors quake, as every moment they face death*
> *just as it slips away."*

Then the Greeks were put to flight and great and brave men
fell from both camps. Gallant leaders rallied their men,
Hector calling for blazing torches to set fire to the ships and
Ajax spurring his men on, shouting,

> *"Men of Argos, faithful companions of Ares, stand up as men,*
> *hold upright the flame of courage...........Forget timidity.*
> *Our freedom is in our own hands."*

And with that, as each man approached with a flaming brand,
he thrust his long lance at him, killing twelve as he stood
breast to breast with them in the rigging.

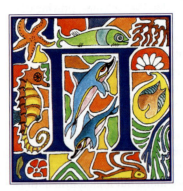

BOOK 16

In tears, Patroclus reached Achilles, who looked askance at his weeping friend, comparing him to a child asking his mother to carry him. Patroclus accused Achilles of having a heart of stone and wondered if he knew of some prophecy of the gods which held him back from the battle. He begged Achilles to lend him his armour, that he might fight, listing the leaders who were wounded, Agamemnon, Odysseus and Diomedes among them.

Achilles admitted that all that kept him from the fray was the grudge he still harboured against Agamemnon. But he realised he could not remain piqued forever and told Patroclus to take his armour and lead his men into battle, for all he could hear were Hector's war cries. He instructed Patroclus to save the ships but not to go on to Troy.

Meanwhile, back on the battlefield, Ajax was in trouble. Hector struck his spear such a blow with his axe that it broke in two, leaving him without a weapon and in no time his ship was in flames. Achilles saw the blaze from his own vessel and urged his friend to put on his armour. And so the faithful Patroclus took up the bronze greaves, the shining breastplate and the great sword and shield of Achilles. The horses of Achilles were yoked to his chariot by Automedon while Achilles rounded up his men. He had brought fifty ships and each had fifty men. Achilles appointed five leaders, Menesthius, Eudorus, Peisander, Phoenix and Alcimedon. He spoke to them, reminding them that they had all been angry at being kept away from battle. Now it was their turn to fight like the brave men they were.

As his troops went to their positions, Achilles, back at his hut, rinsed out a goblet, filled it with wine and poured a libation to Zeus, praying to him to heed his request. This time, he asked for victory for Patroclus. He pleaded with the god to save the ships and send his friend safely back to him. Zeus listened, but granted Achilles only half his wish.

The sight of Patroclus leading Achilles' men on to the field put

Patroclus in the armour of Achilles

terror into the hearts of the Trojans, who thought that it was Achilles himself who had come to join the battle. Patroclus was the first to draw blood and put out a blazing ship. As the Greeks who had taken shelter behind their vessels returned to the fight, confusion reigned. One by one, Trojans fell until Hector and his men took to their horses and retreated in a cloud of dust, Patroclus in hot pursuit, spurring on his gallant steeds, man after man falling under his spear thrusts, as he avenged the deaths of his comrades, until the Trojan Sarpedon turned and leapt from his chariot to meet him face to face.

From his mountain vantage point, Zeus wanted to save Sarpedon, but Hera told him to allow Death and Sleep to do their work. So the two men fought. Patroclus' spear felled Sarpedon's squire and Sarpedon's spear missed Patroclus but felled his horse. Sarpedon's next thrust missed and Patroclus struck Sarpedon near the heart. As the great soldier fell, with his dying breath he called to Glaucus for help. Glaucus, wounded by an arrow from Teucer, prayed to Apollo for strength and the god healed him, allowing him to seek out Hector whom he begged to make a stand and avenge Sarpedon's death.

Over Sarpedon's body the sorrowing Trojans, led by Hector, met the Greeks, strengthened by Patroclus. First the Greeks were under pressure, then the Trojans. Guided by the busy fingers of Zeus, Patroclus' sword whirled, men fell to the ground and Hector turned his horses to flee. Patroclus, his promise to Achilles forgotten, gave chase until, at the very walls of Troy, Apollo ordered him back, telling him that he was not destined to take the city. Then Apollo sent Hector back into the fray, where the warrior, his horses thrashing wildly, had eyes only for Patroclus.

Leaping from his chariot, Patroclus hurled a stone at Hector, which felled his charioteer. As he made to strip the body, seizing it by the feet, Hector jumped down and took hold of his dead charioteer's head. As the Greeks drew around on one side and the Trojans on the other, the two armies met again in fierce conflict. Three times Patroclus charged and killed all around him, but on the fourth he came up against Apollo himself, who struck him, knocking off his helmet and breaking his lance. Patroclus, stunned from the blow, was not quick enough to avoid the weapon of the Trojan Euphorbus and, on his way back to his line, wounded, he was pierced through as Hector lunged with his spear.

When Hector stood over his victim, boasting, the dying Patroclus told him that it was not he alone who had done the deed, but first Zeus and Apollo and Euphorbus after them. As he drew his last breath, he told Hector that he was destined to be slain by Achilles.

BOOK 17

Menelaus stepped forward to remove the body of Patroclus, but Euphorbus claimed the dead man, for he had been first to wound him. When Menelaus refused to give up the body, Euphorbus struck him, but was unable to pierce his armour. Menelaus thrust his own spear through the neck of his enemy, mortally wounding him. Urged by Apollo, Hector and his men charged towards the Greek warrior who was stripping the dead Trojan of his arms. Alarmed at the sight, Menelaus hesitated. Should he stay and reclaim the body of Patroclus and be attacked and surely wounded, if not killed, by Hector, or should he relinquish him and suffer the scorn of his fellow men.

The decision was made quickly as he was confronted by the terrible sight of Hector and his troops. Menelaus retreated, but sought out Ajax, asking for his help in recovering the body of Patroclus for Achilles although it was, by then, stripped of its armour by Hector.

The two men forced Hector to retreat, thus preventing him

from removing the head from the body. Ajax covered Patroclus with his shield as Menelaus stood guard.

Back behind the Trojan lines, Glaucus scorned Hector for his cowardice, not only in failing to claim the body of Patroclus, but also for neglecting to remove Sarpedon's body from the battlefield, leaving it for the Greeks. With that, Hector, riled, decided to put on the armour of Achilles which he had removed from the dead Patroclus. Then, bearing the great man's arms, he addressed his men, offering half his spoils of war for the man who drove Ajax from the field and brought back the body of Patroclus.

So the Trojans charged. Menelaus and Ajax, seeing them coming, called to their own men for help. So once more, the two armies clashed. And, once more, brave men fell on both sides until the Trojans were about to retreat. But Apollo spoke to Aeneas and gave him new heart when he assured him that

Menelaus and Hector over the body of Patroclus

Zeus was still on the side of Troy. The battle raged all day, over the body of Patroclus.

Meanwhile, Achilles' horses mourned their driver, Patroclus. Automedon, in place of the dead man, tried his best to persuade the animals to move, but they stood and grieved beside the chariot. Zeus took pity on them, giving them new spirit and Automedon drove them into the fray, passing the reins to Alcimedon when he found the horses difficult to control.

Hector saw the beautiful animals in harness, pulling Achilles' chariot, and decided to capture them for himself. When Automedon saw him coming, accompanied by Aeneas, he told Alcimedon to stay near him with the chariot. Then he called to the Ajax brothers and Menelaus for help. For a small space of time, those warriors left the dead Patroclus and came to the aid of Automedon and forced Hector to give up his plan.

Back around Patroclus, the furious fight continued. Athena put fresh strength into Menelaus, who immediately killed Podes, a good friend of Hector. Apollo gave the Trojan leader the news, filling him with a desire for vengeance and Zeus, with a mighty thunder clap, let all know whose side he was on. As Greeks fled before the flailing sword of Hector, Menelaus offered a prayer to Zeus, asking him to lift the low cloud which hung over the battlefield, that he might at least see. He wanted to send a messenger to Achilles, to let him know that his friend was dead.

As Zeus answered the prayer and the sun shone, Ajax sent a reluctant Menelaus to look for Antilochus, son of Nestor and order him to take the news to Achilles. On his return to the battle ground, he and Meriones picked up the body of Patroclus and, with the two Ajax brothers gallantly attempting to hold back the enemy, they began to drag it away.

BOOK 18

When Achilles heard of the death of Patroclus from Antilochus, he fell into despair and

"......the pain wrapped itself around him like a black cloud as with both hands he threw fists full of ashes over his head, staining his beautiful face. And the ash settled on his musk scented tunic as the huge man threw himself to the ground, face to the dirt, tearing out his hair. And the slaves which he and Patroclus had captured, cried out in a great voice from the pain which they felt and ran through the doors to Achilles, beating their breasts as they knelt around him."

A weeping Antilochus held tight to Achilles' hands, fearful that he might cut his throat, so wild was his grief.

Then Achilles let out a great cry of anguish, which was heard by his mother, Thetis, who came to him, asking why he wept, when Zeus had done what he prayed for, and allowed the Greeks to suffer terrible hardships.

Little comfort could he gain from that, replied Achilles, when his greatest friend was dead. Now he no longer wished to live, unless he could revenge the death of Patroclus and put Hector to the sword.

Thetis told him that he was destined not to live after the death of Hector. And Achilles saw that he had let down, not only his friend, but his compatriots, over an outburst of anger. Even in

Herhaestos fashioned a shield for Achiles

his grief, however, he saw that what was done, was done. There was no going back. What he had to do was go into battle and slay Hector. However, as he had no armour, Thetis promised to bring him a set at dawn the next day.

In the meantime, the Greeks were hard pressed, trying to keep the body of Patroclus out of Trojan hands. The goddess Iris, watching, went swiftly to Achilles and told him to go into action, even without his armour. As Achilles rose to do her bidding, Athena wrapped him in a mist that shone like gold. When Achilles came to the Greek trench and uttered three great war cries, all the time shimmering bright as flames, the Trojans were filled with terror. Then Hera used her influence to make the sun set early and, as darkness fell, the two armies separated.

Horrified by the appearance of Achilles, the Trojans held a council of war. Polydamas, friend of Hector, advised withdrawing behind the city walls and fighting from the safety of the ramparts at daybreak. Hector scorned the idea. They would all rest for the night and as the sun rose, they would attack the Greek ships with renewed vigour.

In the Greek camp, Patroclus was mourned through the hours of darkness. To the accompaniment of the groaning men, Achilles had the body washed and annointed with precious oils. While this was being done, Thetis went to the smith god, Hephaestus, who was busy at his forge, and begged him to make a set of armour for Achilles. Hephaestus set to work and wrought a wonderful shield for the warrior. He decorated it with the earth, sky, sun, moon and stars; with cities and spectacles of battle, pastoral scenes and dancing maidens, all surrounded by the great river Oceanus. He finished by fashioning a helmet, greaves and breastplate and offered them to Thetis who gathered them all in her arms.

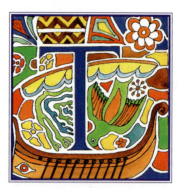

BOOK 19

"In her saffron robes, Dawn rose from the flowing waters of Oceanus, bringing light to both gods and men."

And Thetis went to the Greek ships with the gift of the god Hephaestus, finding Achilles weeping still, arms around the body of his dead friend. When he saw the wonderful armour, the desire for battle rose in him and, as Thetis tended the body with flaming wine and musk to preserve it, he called the men together and the meeting was attended by the wounded Odysseus and Agamemnon.

Achilles rose and addressed the King, expressing a desire to end their quarrel, for the only people who had done well by it were the Trojans and Hector. He suggested that the king call the men to battle to defend their ships. Agamemnon rose. Ate, he said, that personification of moral blindness, had been at work. Just as she had blinded the great Zeus once, on the occasion of the birth of Heracles, so she had impaired his own vision. He would end the feud and pay Achilles his compensation for the loss of Briseis. He ordered his men to prepare themselves for battle. Achilles, not interested in the

Athena hands Achilles his helmet

payment for the moment, agreed, but Odysseus pointed out that the troops had not eaten and should go into the fight well fed. Also, said Odysseus, the men should see the gifts the king intended to give to Achilles and hear Agamemnon swear that he had not taken Briseis to bed.

Achilles, however, wanted to go straight into the fight, while his adrenalin was flowing. The men, he said, could eat after the battle. For himself, food did not interest him while his friend lay dead. Odysseus, however, won the argument. So the gifts of Agamemnon were laid out, a boar was sacrificed to Zeus and the men ate their fill. Briseis, mourning at the sight of the dead Patroclus, was returned to Achilles who, although coaxed by several, including Odysseus, Nestor and Phoenix, refused to eat until he had fought.

The watching Zeus encouraged Athena to go to the help of Achilles and she strengthened him with the food of the gods before he put on his armour. He placed on his head the shining helmet, with its glittering golden plume, taking up his great bronze sword and the wonderful shield fashioned by Hephaestos, along with a spear so heavy that only he could throw it. As his horses were yoked to his chariot, he ordered them to bring him back alive rather than leave him dead as they had Patroclus. With that, one of his horses was given the power of speech by the gods. It warned Achilles of his impending death. But Achilles knew he was soon to die and drove his animals to battle with a resounding cry.

BOOK 20

As the battle began, on Olympus there was a great gathering of gods. Poseidon asked Zeus why they had been summoned and that god replied that while he himself would remain and watch from the mountain, Poseidon and all the gods were allowed to join the battle and fight for either side.

So Hera, Poseidon, Athena, Hermes and Hephaestus left in the direction of the Greek ships and Ares, Apollo, Artemis, Leto and Aphrodite set out to join the Trojan forces. Pandemonium reigned as gods and men fought together. Achilles wanted only to meet Hector. But Apollo encouraged Aeneas to confront him, filling that soldier with courage when his heart failed him. Hera called on Poseidon to go to the aid of Achilles but Poseidon suggested that they left the mortals to battle it out alone. The gods retired once more and Aeneas approached Achilles, who taunted him, asking him if he thought he would become king in Priam's place if he won the fight and reminding him that he had fled from his spear once before.

A proud Aeneas chose to ignore the insults and related his ancestry, which included the boy Ganymedes, cup bearer to

Athena and Artemis joined the battle •

Zeus himself. They could stand there like nagging women or get on with the fight, he said and with that he hurled his spear. The throw did no damage, for it could not pierce the great shield, five layers thick, carried by Achilles and fashioned by Hephaestus. Achilles' spear went through his opponnent's shield but did no harm.

Achilles drew his sword and Aeneas picked up a huge rock but still Achilles came on. At that point Poseidon interfered. He blinded Achilles momentarily, pulling his spear out of his opponent's shield before removing Aeneas from the battle ground. A puzzled Achilles, his sight quickly restored, found his opponent vanished and his great spear lying on the ground in front of him.

Realising that Aeneas was protected by a god, Achilles rallied his men. Hector put heart into his own troops and the battle recommenced. Like Diomedes before him, Achilles was everywhere on the field. Iphiton fell when the spear of Achilles cut his head in half. Demoleon was slain and Hippodamas died, but when Achilles slew Hector's brother, Polydorus, Hector leapt into battle. He let loose his spear at

Achilles but Athena turned it so it flew back to lie useless at Hector's feet. As Achilles responded, Apollo hid Hector and Achilles let fly at nothing.

Swearing to destroy Hector when they met again, Achilles cast his spear and thrust his sword as Trojan after Trojan fell before him, his horses, his chariot and his hands red with the blood of the enemy.

BOOK 21

As Achilles led his men on, he divided the Trojans at the Xanthus river, forcing half across the fields where Hera caused them to be surrounded by a thick mist, while the other half were driven into the river, where the waters ran deep. As soldiers struggled in the current, Achilles leapt in with his sword, slaughtering all about until the river flowed red. In the water he met a certain Lycaon, son of King Priam. This man had been captured not long before by Achilles who sold him in Lemnos to a son of Jason. There a ransom was paid for him by someone he had befriended once. Eventually he had managed to make his way back to Troy, only to find himself unarmed and face to face with Achilles in a river. Lycaon begged for mercy, telling Achilles that he did not have the same mother as Hector, who had killed Patroclus. But Achilles was deaf to his pleading and slew him with his sword, leaving him in the river to be pushed out to sea, food for the fish.

The river however, while Achilles went on to throw a spear at the Trojan Asteropaeus, was not pleased. Asteropaeus wounded Achilles slightly in the arm with one of his weapons and Achilles missed with his throw, his great spear piercing the ground, buried up to half its length. As Asteropaeus tried to remove it, Achilles drew his sword and killed him.

Retreiving his spear, Achilles went to work again, slaying so many men that the river remonstrated with him, telling him to go and fight the Trojans in the fields, for his waters were so full of dead bodies that his way out to sea was blocked. When Achilles refused to listen, the river rose in a great torrent,

throwing bodies up on to dry land and sweeping Achilles off his feet. When the great warrior grasped a tree, its roots were torn from the bank. When Achilles struggled once more to reach dry land, the river rose again in a great wave and Achilles ran before it, the water roaring behind him. If he turned to face it, the

Lycaon begs for Mercy

great wave came crashing down on him, only to be replaced by another. At last Achilles prayed to Zeus and Poseidon and Athena went to encourage him, telling him not to stop fighting and not to return to the ships until Hector was dead.

Achilles set out across the fields which by then were flooded. The river tried once more to stop him, but Hera went to Hephaestus for help, asking him to use the flames from his forge. So Hephaestus did as he was bid, sending flames which burned the bodies of the dead, scorched the fields and set alight to the river itself until it begged for mercy. Hephaestus put out his fires, the river flowed more gently and the gods were in dispute once more.

To the amusement of Zeus, Ares confronted Athena, striking her and she brought him to his knees by hurling a rock. As Aphrodite went to the aid of the War god, Athena hit her and she fell, joining Ares on the ground. Poseidon challenged Apollo to a fight and Apollo refused, only to be mocked by Artemis, his twin sister. Hera struck Artemis, the goddess of hunting, who ran to Olympus, leaving her bow and arrows behind. These were collected by Leto, mother of the heavenly twins, as Artemis sobbed in the arms of Zeus. Apollo set out for Troy and the rest of the gods, their quarrels over, gathered on Olympus.

From the battlements of Troy, King Priam saw Achilles gettting the better of his men. He ordered the gates of the city to be opened, in order that his troops might reach the safety of the city. As the men rushed across the open fields towards Troy, Achilles and his men on their heels, Apollo instilled courage into the heart of Agenor who stood to meet his enemy, wishing he could turn and run, but realising that death would come to him just the same, for Achilles would seek him out. His spear thrust hit Achilles on the shin, but could not pierce the greaves fashioned by Hephaestus. As Achilles went into the attack, Apollo hid Agenor in cloud, removed him from the spot and took his place. Perfectly disguised as Agenor, Apollo ran, leading Achilles a merry dance across the plain as the Trojan troops reached the safety of the city and the great gates were closed.

BOOK 22

Only Hector remained outside the gates of Troy. Achilles, in a rage when he discovered Apollo's trick, raced back to the city, the sight of him filling the watching King Priam with terror, for he had already lost two sons that day, Lycaon and Polydorus. Priam begged Hector to return to safety, within the walls, but even when he was joined by his wife, who added her pleas to his, all was in vain. Hector stood his ground, realising that he should have taken the advice of Polydorus and ordered the withdrawal of the troops earlier, when they could have fought from the city walls, but knowing that his only option was to fight and either win gloriously or die with honour.

Achilles approached, his armour blazing in the sun and

Hector's courage failed him. He turned and ran, Achilles after him. Three times around the city walls the two raced, watched by the gods. Zeus sighed, wishing to save Hector's life but allowing Athena the freedom to do whatever she thought best. On and on ran the two warriors until Zeus balanced death on his golden scales, Hector's on one side and that of Achilles on the other. Down fell the scales on Hector's side and his fate was sealed. Athena allowed Achilles time to recover his breath while she went to Hector disguised as his brother, Deiphobus, advising him to turn and stand up to Achilles. Assuming he had the help of his brother, Hector called out to Achilles. He was going to fight him, he said, but he guaranteed that, if he won, he would not harm Achilles' body. He would only strip it of its armour before handing it over. He asked if Achilles would do the same for him.

Achilles was not interested in making any sort of deal and went straight into battle, flinging his spear at his enemy, who managed to dodge it. The weapon was at once returned to Achilles by Athena, unseen by Hector who threw his own weapon, taunting Achilles as he did. He missed, but had lost his spear and he called to Deiphobus for another lance. When he discovered that his brother was missing, he realised that he had been tricked by the gods. He drew his sword and charged forward, but Achilles' spear struck him in the only gap in his armour, at the throat. As Hector fell, Achilles spoke. When Hector had stripped the body of Patroclus, he told him, he had no thought for Achilles. So now, his corpse would be thrown to the dogs.

Hector begged Achilles to give his body to his father, who would pay handsomely for it. But Achilles would not listen to his pleas. When the Trojan leader had breathed his last, Achilles stripped him of his armour and his men stood gazing

at the body, marvelling at its size as they thrust their spears at it. And that was not all. Achilles cut a slit in the feet of the dead Hector, inserted leather thongs and secured the body behind his chariot.

With Hector's head dragging in the dirt behind him, Achilles drove away in a cloud of dust. On the walls of Troy, Hector's mother, Hecuba, tore at her hair in distress and Priam had to be held back by his friends as he wept for his son. As the people mourned, the cries of sorrow reached the ears of Andromache. Climbing on to the city wall to see what had happened, she saw Hector's body being dragged around the town and she fell, fainting, to the ground.

The death of Hector

BOOK 23

Back at the Greek camp, Achilles dragged the body of Hector three times around that of Patroclus, before releasing it and flinging it to the ground. While his men feasted on roasted ox, sheep, goats and pigs, Achilles, reluctant to leave the remains of his friend, nevertheless dined, as requested, with Agamemnon, refusing to wash the blood of Hector from himself, until the funeral was over.

That night, as he lay beside the sea and slept, Achilles was visited by the spirit of Patroclus, which begged him to make sure their bones would be buried together. And at dawn, wood was collected for the funeral pyre. Achilles and his men put on their armour. Charioteers yoked their horses. In grave procession, the chariots set out, followed by myriad foot soldiers and after them came Achilles, supporting the shorn head of his friend, Patroclus, as they made their way to the appointed place.

The wood was piled to a great height, the body laid on top, a lock of Achilles' hair in its hands. Achilles dismissed all the troops except for a few. Sheep and cattle were sacrificed and their carcasses placed on the pyre, along with honey and oil.

Two of Patroclus' dogs were killed and placed on the mound by Achilles, together with four horses. Then Achilles killed twelve Trojans, adding their bodies to the pyre before setting it alight. When it refused to burn, Achilles prayed to the Winds and the fire caught, burning strongly all night as a weeping Achilles poured libations of wine on the earth.

The next morning, after an exhausted Achilles had fallen into a deep sleep, he was woken by Agamemnon. Achilles asked the king and other leaders to douse the fire with wine and place the bones of Patroclus in a golden casket. Stones were laid around the pyre and inside them an earth barrow built as a monument. Then Achilles held Funeral Games beside the memorial, in honour of his friend. The men sat in a great ring, forming an arena.

A chariot race was held first. The contestants were Eumelus, Diomedes, Menelaus, Meriones and Antilochus. The latter was the young son of Nestor, who gave the youth the benefit of his experience with some wise advice before the race. Names were placed in a helmet and Antilochus drew the first starting place, followed by Eumelus, Menelaus, Meriones and finally Diomedes.

All were together until they turned, when Eumelus led, Diomedes just behind. Apollo sent the whip flying from the hand of Diomedes, but Athena retrieved it and went on to damage Eumelus' chariot and he was thrown to the ground, the breath knocked out of him. So Diomedes led, with Menelaus not far behind, and after them Antilochus. Where the track narrowed, Antilochus drove his horses to one side and managed to pass Menelaus.

Into the arena came Diomedes, and his prize was a tripod and a woman, clever with her fingers. Next to arrive was Antilochus, who claimed the second prize, a pregnant mare and the third prize, a bright tureen, went to Menelaus. Two talents of gold were offered to Meriones, who came in fourth. When Eumelus came in to the arena with his horses, pulling his own chariot, Achilles felt so sorry for him that he suggested that he took the second prize, for he was the greatest charioteer. Antilochus at once protested, refusing to give up the mare and telling Achilles to give up some of his own treasure, if he wished to reward Eumelus.

Achilles, smiling, gave Eumelus his bronze breastplate, whereupon Menelaus accused Antilochus of cutting across in front of his horses. Antilochus begged forgiveness and offered Menelaus the mare. Menelaus gallantly accepted the apology and returned the animal to Antilochus. Achilles awarded the fifth prize, a two handled pan, to Nestor, for he knew the old soldier was unable to compete in any of the events.

The next contest was a boxing match, the winner to receive a mule and the loser a mug. Epeius, a champion boxer, laid his

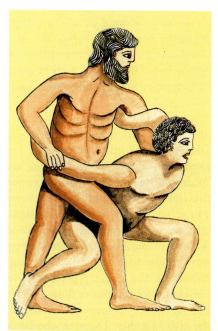

Ajax and Odysseus wrestle

hand on the mule and dared someone to fight him for it. Euryalus, a cousin of Diomedes, took up the challenge and the hands of the competitors were bound with leather strips. For a while the fight was even, until Euryalus lost his concentration and was knocked senseless.

The third event was wrestling and Ajax and Odysseus met in combat. Neither man could throw the other. The contest was so equal that it was declared a draw amd both men won a great cauldron.

The three prizes for the foot race were a silver bowl, a plump ox and half a talent of gold, in that order. Lesser Ajax, Odysseus and the young Antilochus took part. Lesser Ajax led all the way, followed closely by Odysseus, who sent up a hasty prayer to Athena just before the finish and Ajax tripped. So Odysseus took the silver bowl, Ajax the ox and when Antilochus claimed his award he paid such a pleasant tribute to Odysseus that Achilles added another half talent to his prize.

The next event was a fight between two men, wearing helmets and armed with a shield and long spear. Great Ajax and Diomedes took up this challenge. The spear of Ajax pierced Diomedes' shield but got no further. Diomedes thrust his spear and its point reached his opponent's neck, whereupon the fight was stopped by the crowd and the reward of a Thracian sword, which Achilles had taken from the unfortunate Asteropaeus, went to Diomedes.

A lump of pig iron, considered of great value at that time, went to the winner of the next contest, the discus throw. Although the great Ajax competed, the prize went to Polypoetes for his mighty fling.

For the archery contest, Achilles tied a pigeon, by its foot, to the mast of a ship. The man who hit the fluttering bird, would win a set of double headed axes, while the man who could pierce the string would have a set of single headed axes. Teucer shot first and hit the string, thus freeing the pigeon. Meriones took up his bow and shot. His arrow went right through the bird, landing back at his feet and the bird fell dead to the ground.

The javelin throw was the last event. King Agamemnon rose to compete, as did Meriones. The tactful Achilles rose at once , saying everyone knew that the king was the champion at this competition and he awarded the first prize, a cauldron, to Agamemnon. Meriones was content to take a spear as his award.

BOOK 24

The games over, Achilles was not at peace. He still mourned his friend and day after day he dragged the body of Hector, preserved by the gods with oils and ointments, around the memorial mound. By the twelfth day, Apollo had had enough. He accused his fellow immortals of taking the side of a pitiless Achilles, whereas Hector had often offered sacrifice to them, which they had accepted. Hera retorted that Hector was simply an ordinary mortal, but Achilles was son of a goddess, Thetis. Zeus put a stop to the quarrel and ordered Thetis to be brought before him. He told the goddess to go to her son and say that Zeus and the rest of the gods were not happy with him. Zeus also sent Iris to Priam, with a request that he go to Achilles and offer a ransom for the body of Hector.

Thetis approached the melancholy Achilles and Iris the aged and grieving Priam. Achilles agreed to accept a ransom and Priam, against the advice of Hecuba, who thought he would be slain by Achilles, collected treasure fit for a ransom from his coffers before setting out for the Greek camp. First the citizens of Troy tried to stop him, and then his sons. But Priam was adamant and while the horses were being yoked to the chariots, Hecuba came to her husband with wine for him to offer to Zeus, with a prayer for a sign in the form of an eagle. If they recieved no sign, Priam agreed not to go. When the libation was poured and a great bird swooped over the city, Priam set out.

Hermes was dispatched by Zeus to protect the old king. Pretending to be a servant of Achilles, Hermes assured Priam that the gods had protected the body of his son. Hector's wounds had healed and his body was unmarked. At the Greek wall, Hermes put the sentries to sleep. When Priam and his chariot came near to Achilles' hut, which was surrounded by a protective fence, Hermes himself opened the great door and let the king in to the enclosure.

Priam fell on his knees before an astonished Achilles, begging for the body of his son. "*I have come to redeem him from you and I bring unmeasured ransom*," he said. These words are an echo of the words of another father, who, at the beginning of the book, begged for his daughter. "*Chryses came to redeem his daughter bringing unmeasured ransom*", wrote Homer. The king then kissed the hand of his enemy, the hand that had killed so many of his sons. He asked Achilles to think of his own father who at least knew he was still alive and had something to look forward to. Priam said his had been the best sons in the kingdom and now he had not one left that was worth while. Hector had been the last of them.

Achilles was so deeply moved by the old man's words that the two wept together for some moments. Then Achilles asked Priam to sit for a while, but the old man would not, while his son lay uncared for in the huts of the enemy. Achilles quick temper rose and he told the king not to provoke him. He said he would have given Hector back without any pleading on the part of Priam, and rushed out of the room. The old king was seated and the ransom inspected, while Achilles, asking the spirit of Patroclus to forgive him, had Hector's body annointed and wrapped in fine linen.

Returning to Priam, Achilles told him that his son was ready to be taken back and asked him to sup with him, pointing out that when Artemis killed Niobe's daughters and Apollo her sons, after nine days of mourning even Niobe had to eat. So a sheep was killed and roasted, eaten with bread and washed down with wine. Priam was given a bed for the night, but before he went to sleep, Achilles asked him how many days the Trojans would be in mourning for Hector, for he would refrain from continuing with the war for that length of time.

Priam replied that they would mourn his son for nine days and bury him on the tenth. On the eleventh day they would build the barrow and fighting could begin again on the twelfth. With that agreed, Priam was left to sleep, but Hermes came to him in the night and suggested that

Priam and a ransom for Hector

he leave quietly. He may have an agreement with Achilles, said the god, and he had paid a great ransom for Hector, but his sons would have to pay far more for Priam as well, if Agamemnon found him there.

The first person to see Priam approaching Troy was his daughter, Cassandra, who was keeping watch on the city walls. Her cries were heard by the people, who poured out of the city gates and surrounded the king and Hector's bier, wailing and weeping, while Hecuba tore out her hair in grief.

Once in the city, the body was taken to the palace, where Andromache led the mourning, joined by Hecuba and then by Helen. How she wished she had not lived, said Helen, weeping. In all the years she had been in Troy, Hector had never said an unkind word to her. More than that, when others had hurled insults at her, Hector had spoken in her defence, addressing her gently.

King Priam ordered the building of the funeral pyre. It took the people nine days to collect the wood and on the tenth day they burned the body. On the eleventh day they quenched the fire with wine, took the bones, placed them in a golden casket and buried them. They constructed the barrow quickly, incase the Greeks decided to attack early, before going back to the city and feasting.

So they buried Hector, the great warrior.

Homer brings the Iliad to an end here. But, of course, that was not the end of the war, which was finally won by the Greeks. Apollodorus, a Greek historian of the 1st century AD, tells us that Memnon brought an army of Ethiopians to side with Troy against the enemy. Memnon killed Antilochus, only to be slain in turn by Achilles. An arrow from Paris, guided by Apollo, finally killed Achilles when it pierced the only mortal part of him, his heel. Ajax and Odysseus competed for his armour.

Games were held in his honour and his bones, together with those of Patroclus, were buried, according to Apollodorus, on the island of Leuce, but Homer says otherwise, as you shall see.

Part 3

A Simple Re-telling of The Odyssey

> *Much have I seen and known; cities of men*
> *And manners, climates, councils, governments,*
> *Myself not least, but honour'd of them all;*
> *And drunk delight of battle with my peers,*
> *Far on the ringing plains of windy Troy.*
> *I am a part of all that I have met;*
> *Yet all experience is an arch wherethro'*
> *Gleams that untravell'd world, whose margin fades*
> *For ever and ever when I move.*

> *Alfred Lord Tennyson 'Ulysses'(Odysseus)*

The adventures and misfortunes that befell the Greek leaders as they struggled to return to their homeland after the Trojan war inspired the imagination of the epic poets. The poems they wrote were called 'nosti', meaning 'songs of return'. So the story of Odysseus is one such epic, for the Odyssey deals with the heroic efforts of the warrior to reach his home in Ithaca. The journey took him ten years.

BOOK 1

Homer begins the Odyssey, as he did the Iliad, with a call to a Muse, appealing for inspiration in the telling of a tale. A tale of a much travelled man who, after he had crushed the holy citadel of the Trojans, wandered the world. 'A man who endured many calamities on the high seas, living only to reach his homeland, together with his companions, unharmed.' The man was Odysseus.

The Greeks who fought in the ten year long war with Troy had reached home, with one exception. The nymph, Calypso, had imprisoned Odysseus in a cave on a remote island. The gods met on Olympus and Zeus voiced his thoughts to them. He had been thinking of Aegisthus, who, while Agamemnon had been absent for so many years fighting the Trojans, took the king's wife and then murdered him when he returned from the war. And how Agamemnon's son, Orestes, had taken his revenge and put Aegisthus to the sword.

Athena said that Aegisthus only had himself to blame. She herself was more sorry for Odysseus, languishing on an island far from home. Why, she asked Zeus, was he so against him?

It was not he, but Poseidon, said Zeus, who had taken a dislike to Odysseus, after that hero had blinded Polyphemus, the one-eyed giant. It was the great god of the sea who encouraged Calypso to keep Odysseus, for Polyphemus was his son by the nymph Phorcys.

'Let us put our heads together then,' said Zeus, 'and consider how Odysseus can return. Poseidon will abandon his hatred towards him, for he can do nothing alone, with his fellow gods against him.'

As a result of the discussion, Hermes, the messenger god, was sent to Calypso on the island of Ogygia, to notify her that the gods wished Odysseus to resume his journey home. Athena went to Ithaca, home of Odysseus, to encourage his son to look for news of his father from Nestor, disguising herself as a warrior named Mentes.

The youth Telemachus welcomed Athena to the palace of Odysseus, King of Ithaca, saying, when she asked, that his mother had told him he was the son of Odysseus and he hoped he was, but that no one was sure of his own

A Muse

lineage. He took her to the great hall, sitting her down and offering wine and food. They were surrounded by the suitors, men who were vying with each other to pay court to Penelope, wife of Odysseus, certain that the king was dead and wishing to take over his lands, property and wife. And in the meanwhile, said Telemachus, they were feasting and making merry at his expense. They would all be gone in a moment, he assured the goddess, if they once caught sight of Odysseus.

Athena told the despondent Telemachus that she was there with the news that Odysseus was alive and she suggested that he gather a ship and crew and sail for Pylos, to speak with the aged Nestor and to go afterwards to Sparta, to see Menelaus. These two would give him news of his father. In the meantime the disguised Athena proposed he should find a way to get rid of his mother's unwanted admirers. She told him to grow up and become as brave as Orestes. With that, she disappeared, and Telemachus realised that he had been in the presence of a goddess.

Filled with new heart, Telemachus found his mother weeping, for the minstrels were singing a sad song. She asked them to stop, for it was a song of the return from Troy and the sufferings inflicted on the Greeks by the gods. Telemachus ordered his mother to her room, saying that the minstrels had a right to sing, for it was not their fault that the words of the song were true. The blame lay with Zeus.

Surprised at her son's new and sudden command of himself, Penelope withdrew and Telemachus turned to the suitors. They could feast for the moment, he said, but in the morning they would attend a meeting, when he would insist on their departure.

BOOK 2

Early next morning, the heralds summoned the elders of Ithaca to a meeting. Old Aegyptius was first to speak. His son had sailed with Odysseus and been killed by Polyphemus. Aegyptius wondered who had called the gathering, the first since Odysseus had left. Was there news of Ithaca's army returning?

Telemachus rose and admitted to calling the meeting. No, he said, he had no news of the army to impart. He had called the men together for a more personal reason. He was being eaten out of house and home by those courting his mother. They were feasting their way through his wealth and were simply encouraged by the people of the town. He begged to be allowed to grieve alone and in peace for his father.

One of the suitors, Antinous, got to his feet. It was not their fault, he said, but Penelope's. For years she had kept them waiting, weaving a piece of work on her loom, saying that when it was finished, she would choose a husband. But each night, they had discovered, she unravelled the day's work. She might be very beautiful and clever, but she had misused her brains in this case. Telemachus should cast her out of the house and insist she marry. They would not go home until she had chosen one of them.

Telemachus refused and the watching Zeus sent a sign in the form of two eagles. The birds swung down together from their mountain home and swooped over the crowd, biting and scratching at each other. An aged soothsayer, seeing the omen, stood and addressed the crowd.

The portent was not good, he said. It would not be long before Odysseus returned and it did not bode well for the suitors. The old man reminded the assembly that he had foretold correctly that Odysseus would be late in returning and that no one would recognise him when he did.

Eurymachus rose to his feet. Many birds fought in the air, he said. It was normal. There was no sign. Odysseus was dead.

Telemachus must prepare his mother for a wedding and they would all stay, feasting on his wealth, until she had chosen a husband.

Telemachus would not speak of the matter again. He anounced that he was going to Pylos to make enquiries about his father. If he discovered that

Penelope at her loom

he was dead, then he would return and choose a husband for his mother.

The next to speak was Mentor, a friend of Odysseus and he accused the citizens gathered there of sitting in silence and giving no thought to Odysseus and his estate which was being wasted by the suitors. The meeting was broken up when it was suggested by Euenor's son that even Odysseus would be in trouble if he tried to remove the men from his house.

So the suitors returned to the palace of Odysseus to pay court once more to the faithful Penelope and Telemachus sat by the sea and prayed to Athena, for he had neither found a ship in which to sail to Pylos, nor had he got rid of those who were paying court to his mother and feeding on his stores like parasites.

Athena came to him, disguised as Mentor and filling him with courage, telling him that if he had a drop of his father's blood in him, then he would show neither weakness nor cowardice. Most men do not resemble their fathers at all, she said. Most of them were worse but a few, better. She told him to go and collect provisions for his journey and she herself would find a crew and a vessel.

When he returned to his father's home, Telemachus found the suitors preparing a feast to which Antinous invited him. Telemachus refused and amid jeers he left their company and went to his father's store rooms. There he asked his old nurse, Eurycleia, to help him gather provisions which he would collect that night. He asked Euricleia not to tell anyone, for several days, that he had left Ithaca, not even his mother.

The busy Athena, in the meantime, disguised as Telemachus, found a crew and a ship. By nightfall Telemachus himself had ordered the provisions to be put aboard and they set sail while it was still dark.

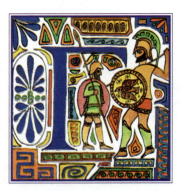

BOOK 3

When Telemachus landed at Pylos, he found the people feasting. They had sacrificed bulls in honour of Poseidon and the young Telemachus had to be encouraged once more by Athena, in the guise of Mentor, to approach the famous old warrior, Nestor, who was seated with his sons in the middle of the revellers. The visitors were welcomed, seated and offered food and wine, before Nestor asked them who they were and where they had come from.

They came from Ithaca, said Telemachus, in search of news of his father. Certain that he was dead, the young man asked Nestor not to hide the truth from him, however painful. Immediately, Nestor recalled the terrible long war with Troy. He remembered the fall of Patroclus, Ajax and Achilles. He spoke of the great deeds of Odysseus, remarking on the likeness between father and son. He remembered the fall of Troy and the quarrel which broke out between Agamemnon and Menelaus. Agamemnon had wanted to stay and sacrifice to Athena but Menelaus wanted to leave for home at once. While they argued, half the men made for the ships and set sail, along with their prisoners and spoils of war, Nestor and his troops among them. But even among those who sailed, there was disagreement, and one ship turned and went back. It was Odysseus and his men. The ships of Nestor and Diomedes carried on, to be joined by Menelaus at Lesbos. Diomedes eventually dropped anchor at Argos and Nestor reached Pylos safely. He had little first hand news of those left behind, but had heard that the Myrmidons were safely home, guided by the son of Achilles, and the Cretans, under Idomenus, had reached home also. Everyone, he said, had heard how Agamemnon fared when he returned, for he was killed by Aegisthus, the murder revenged by Orestes.

Nestor had also heard of the suitors who were paying court to Penelope on Ithaca and living off the lands of Odysseus. Perhaps Odysseus would return one day, he said, for Athena loved him. Telemachus thought that would never be and asked Nestor to relate how Agamemnon had died and why Menelaus had not been there to save him.

So Nestor told the young man how, while he and Menelaus were on their way back, Aegisthus had

Telemachus and Nestor

courted Agamemnon's wife, Clytaemnestra. When Nestor and Menelaus reached Sounion, Menelaus' helmsman dropped dead and Menelaus stopped to bury him while Nestor carried on towards home. When Menelaus eventually left Sounion, his fleet was split in two during bad weather, one group of ships being driven towards Crete, while the remaining ships, commanded by Menelaus, were driven to Egypt. So he was not there to help his brother, Agamemnon, when Aegisthus murdered him and took over the throne of Mycenae. Eight years later, the young Orestes returned from Athens and took his revenge and it was only then that Menelaus reached home.

Nestor suggested that Telemachus go and speak to Menelaus, for he had more recently returned from abroad and his news would be more up to date. In the meantime, he invited the young man to sleep in his home. The disguised Athena announced that she would sleep on board the ship, turned into an eagle and flew away, to the amazement of all, who realised that Telemachus had the gods on his side.

The next morning, Nestor sacrificed a calf to Athena. Telemachus was bathed, oiled and dressed in fine linen before he joined Nestor to eat the roasted meat. When they had quenched their thirst with wine, Telemachus was given a chariot and horses driven by Peisistratus, Nestor's son, to make his way to Lacedaemon and the palace of Menelaus.

BOOK 4

Celebrations were in order at the palace of King Menelaus, for his daughter was promised to wed the son of Achilles while his son, Megapenthes, was marrying a girl from Sparta. When Telemachus and Peisistratus arrived, they were welcomed, bathed and invited to the feast. Later, said Menelaus, they could tell him who they were. The two were amazed at the wealth displayed all around them. When the king heard their comments he explained that his riches did not bring him much pleasure, for he had been through many hardships to bring them home and, in his absence, his brother had been murdered. He missed the company of his friends who had died during the long war, but most of all he missed Odysseus. He said his family was probably mourning for him; Penelope, his wife, together with Telemachus, his son who had been a baby when the war started.

The king was mystified when Telemachus began to weep and wail and while he was wondering what to say, Helen, his wife, joined them, asking who their guests were, for the young man was amazingly like Odysseus. Menelaus, when he thought about it, had to agree and Peisistratus explained who

Telemachus was and that he had been sent by Nestor to ask for advice concerning matters at home. Soon, Helen, Telemachus, Menelaus and Peisistratus were weeping together at the thought of Odysseus. But after the king had promised to speak to Telemachus the next day, Helen slipped a potion into their wine which made them forget their sorrow for a while as she told them the tale of a daring deed undertaken by Odysseus. She told them of how he had whipped himself until he looked like a beaten slave. Dressed in rags, he had managed to slip into Troy unnoticed, to learn the plans of the Trojan leaders.

The wooden horse

Menelaus recalled how they had all managed to get into the city in a wooden horse. He and Diomedes, sitting with the rest of the army in the horse, had wanted to cry out and answer at once when they heard Helen calling to them from outside, but Odysseus had stopped them and saved them from death. And with that, they all retired for the night.

The next morning Telemachus related the problem of Penelope's suitors and begged Menelaus for news of his father. Menelaus told him a story. He had been held up in Egypt for some time when he had been blown off course on his way back from Troy. He was on the island of Pharos, at the mouth of the Nile, where the weather kept him from sailing and he was running out of supplies. There, a goddess took pity on him. She was Eidothee, daughter of Proteus, a powerful sea god. If Menelaus could catch him, she advised, the god would tell him how to sail away safely and also give him news of home. With the help of Eidothee, a trap was laid and Proteus was caught. He told Menelaus he should have made a rich sacrifice to Zeus before he left, if he had wanted to reach home with no trouble. As it was, he would have to navigate the Nile again and make the offering before he could set out once more for his homeland When Menelaus asked for news of his companions, the god said that only two commanders died on the way home and one was alive but a prisoner. Ajax had been shipwrecked and Agamemnon, although he reached home, had been killed, along with all his men, by Aegisthus. Menelaus wept for his brother, then asked for news of the third commander. The third, said Proteus, was Odysseus, who was without his ship and kept prisoner on an island, by Calypso.

His story over, Menelaus invited Telemachus to stay for some time in his palace and to accept the gift of three horses and a

chariot. Telemachus begged to be allowed to leave immediately and return to Ithaca. He thanked him his for his generosity but explained that horses would not thrive on his island. So Menealus gave him a precious bowl of silver and gold.

In the meantime however, in Ithaca the suitors learned that Telemachus had gone to Pylos in secret and they hatched a plan to ambush his ship on its way back. Penelope heard of the plot. She herself had not known that her son had left to discover news of his father. In great distress she took to her bed, refusing to eat or drink until Athena took pity on her and sent her a message in a dream, letting her know that her son would be safe. At the same time, Antinous and the suitors put out to sea to wait for Telemachus.

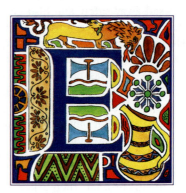

BOOK 5

The gods were gathered on Olympus. Athena reminded Zeus of Odysseus' predicament and of Telemachus, who was to be assassinated as he returned to Ithaca. Zeus sent Hermes once more to convey his wishes to Calypso and he told Athena to use her own powers to save Telemachus. Hermes sped to the far island of Ogygia and found the beautiful Calypso in her cave in front of a roaring fire, singing as she worked at her loom. The nymph welcomed him and after a meal of ambrosia washed down with nectar, he relayed the command of the god of gods, saying that a man had been washed ashore who had spent nine years fighting at Troy. He was destined to reach home and was not to be kept on the island. Calypso complained that a goddess was always thwarted if she wanted to sleep with a mortal. Iasion had been struck dead by Zeus for lying with Demeter and Orion killed by Artemis for loving the goddess of the Dawn. Now it was her turn. But promising to allow Odysseus to leave, she went and found him weeping by the sea, longing for home. She would give him food, clothing and a fair wind, she said, if he would fell the trees and build himself a boat.

Odysseus suspected a trap and extracted a promise from Calypso that she had no plans to destroy him. Back in the cave, she warned him that if he knew of the appalling hardships he would undergo on his way back, he would never leave her island. But Odysseus said he had endured such terrible things in war and on the sea that a few more would make no difference to him.

The next day, with tools supplied by Calypso, Odysseus began the building of his vessel. He cut twenty trees and fashioned the craft. He made a mast and rudder and Calypso supplied material for a sail. Five days later he put to sea with a store of fresh water and wine, grain and meat. Navigating by the stars, he sailed for seventeen days, until he came in sight of the land of the Phaecians. But before he could reach the shore a terrible storm blew up. He lost his oars, the mast broke and he was thrown out of the ship. Somehow he struggled back on board and was tossed here and there on huge waves, out of control until the sea goddess Leucothoe showed some compassion. She boarded the boat and gave Odysseus a veil. He was to take off his clothes, wrap the cloth around himself and swim for the land.

Odysseus saw how far he was from shore and decided to remain with his vessel, but a huge wave wrecked the boat, so he obeyed the instructions of the goddess, wrapped the veil around himself and leaped into the sea.

For two days he struggled in stormy waters and the third day dawned calm. Odysseus came near to land but there was nowhere he could get a foot to the shore, for he could see only great sharp rocks. Caught in the surf he was hurled against them by a wave and as Athena helped him find a hold, he lost the skin from his hands before letting go, to fall into the sea once more, searching again for a place to get ashore. At last he came to the mouth of a river and was able to reach calm water and gain dry land. Exhausted, he lay for a while before climbing up into a wood where he found shelter under two

Odysseus built himself a boat

olive trees. There, where the foliage was thick and wind and rain could not penetrate, he covered himself with leaves and Athena caused him to fall into a deep asleep.

BOOK 6

While Odysseus slept, Athena went to the palace of Alcinous, king of the Phaecians, where his daughter, Nausicaa, lay asleep. Athena disguised herself as a close friend of Nausicaa and spoke to the girl in her sleep, suggesting that they go together, the next morning, to the river to wash their clothes.
Early on the next day, Nausicaa's father supplied her with the wagon she requested, in which to take her garments for washing. Accompanied by her two maids, with the cart full of clothing and a picnic packed by her mother, the girl set out. The three maidens washed and rinsed the clothes, bathed themselves and ate and drank. They played beside the river as the washing dried in the sun and, when one of the maids dropped a ball thrown by Nausicaa, she shouted and so woke the sleeping Odysseus.
Naked, covered in dried sea salt, holding a leafy branch in front of him for modesty's sake, Odysseus was a frightening

sight. The maids fled but encouraged by Athena, Nausicaa remained. Struck by her beauty, Odysseus told of his ordeal in the sea and begged her to direct him to the town and give him something to cover himself with before he went on his way.

Nausicaa called her maids back and under her orders they provided him with food and clothing after he had bathed in the river. Athena made him look more handsome than ever, and Nausicaa told her maids that she wouldn't mind him as a husband.

When all were ready to return, Nausicaa told Odysseus that he could walk with them until they were approaching the town.

Then, to avoid gossiping tongues, he must wait outside the walls and give them time to reach the palace. Then he could enter and ask his way to the royal residence. There he should approach her mother and get her sympathy if he wished to reach his homeland.

When Nausicaa had left, Odysseus sat as instructed and prayed to Athena that the Phaecians would look kindly and graciously on him.

*Odysseus holds
a branch
for modesty*

BOOK 7

When Nausicaa reached home she went to her rooms and after a while Odysseus started out for the town. He asked directions to the palace from a young girl who, unknown to him, was Athena in disguise. She offered to accompany him, for she said the people did not take too kindly to strangers. So the two walked through the town and the goddess made Odysseus invisible to all eyes except her own.

When they reached the palace, Athena told him to go straight to the queen, Arete, whose ancestor was Poseidon. Not only was Arete queen, she was also a very wise woman and much loved by her husband and the people. With those words, Athena left him and Odysseus approached Nausicaa's home with much trepidation, for he was overawed by its beauty. It was decorated with silver, bronze, enamel and gold and rich with wonderfully woven fabrics. The gardens, watered by two springs, were sweet with abundant fruit and a wealth of vegetables.

Odysseus entered, going at once into the great hall, still invisible to all until he reached the queen who, with king and counsellors, was offering libations to Hermes before retiring.

He knelt before her and begged for help from her and her people, to return to his own land.

Everyone sat in bewildered silence at the sudden appearance of Odysseus until one of the elders rose and suggested that the king should not allow a stranger to kneel in the dust, but to offer him a seat, along with some wine and food.

Alcinous at once recovered himself and, when Odysseus was served, they made a libation to Zeus and drank together before the king addressed them. Still uncertain of the stranger who had appeared so abruptly in their midst, Alcinous suggested that they entertain their guest the next day before looking into the matter of his journey home. If he was a god, he said, then that was something new for until then the immortals had appeared to them, or attended their feastings, without a disguise.

Odysseus replied. They could see that he was no god, he said. Indeed, he was the sorriest of humans and could tell them a long tale of woe. But he was hungry for all that and asked to be allowed to eat and sleep before arrangements were made, the next day, for his voyage home.

With that, all withdrew with the exception of the king and queen. Arete had recognized the clothes Odysseus was wearing, for she had helped to make them, so was curious as to who he was. In answer to her numerous questions, Odysseus explained that he had been shipwrecked and washed up on the island of Ogygia. There he had been cared for by Calypso but not allowed to leave until eight years had passed. When he, perhaps by orders of Zeus, had been allowed to build himself a boat and set sail, he had been shipwrecked once more after seventeen days at sea.

Odysseus related his difficulties in getting ashore once he had neared their land, eventually being washed up by the river bed, where he had fallen asleep in a small wood, sheltered by two trees. When he awoke, said Odysseus, it was to see their daughter, playing with her maids. She was kind enough to help him. When Alcinous suggested that his daughter should have

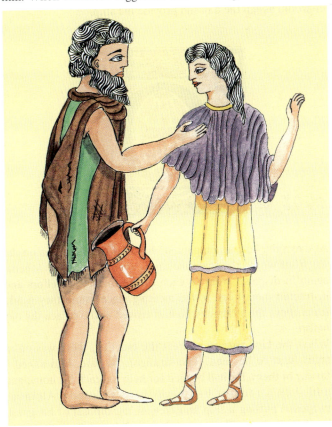

Odysseus asks the way to the palace

brought him to the palace herself, Odysseus explained that he had not wanted to compromise her.

The king, impressed by Odysseus, would have been content to see him as a son in law but, if he wanted to get home, he said, he would assign the day and provide the ship.

BOOK 8

At dawn the king accompanied Odysseus to the square on the sea front where the town meetings were held, while Athena, again in disguise, went to each of the town counsellors and instructed them to go to the meeting place where they would learn about the stranger who had arrived at the palace the day before.

When the king rose to address the meeting, there was not a spare seat to be seen. The stranger, he said, had asked a favour of them. He had begged for help to reach his homeland and such a request had never been refused. Alcinous proposed putting a ship and crew at the diposal of his guest, but first they would entertain him with feasting, contests and the songs of the minstrel, Demodocus.

So the ship was prepared and launched and the people gathered in the palace for the banquet. The minstrel tuned his lyre and began his song. It spoke of a quarrel between Achilles and Odysseus and, as he listened, Odysseus tried to hide his tears. But his sighs were heard by Alcinous, who tactfully suggested going outside, to watch the sporting contests.

After they had enjoyed the spectacles of racing, jumping, boxing, wrestling and discus throwing, someone noticed how well built Odysseus was and asked him to join in their games. Odysseus replied that he was too upset and had suffered to much, to think of participating. To which a certain Euryalus retorted that he could see that the stranger was no sportsman.

Stung into a sharp reply, Odysseus said that a person cannot be judged by his looks. One could be handsome and yet a bad speaker. On the other hand, someone you might never notice could be a wonderful orator. Euryalus was quite good looking yet had no brains. And with that retort, Odysseus picked out the largest of the discs, one never used for throwing and hurled it. It went further than any and the distance was measured by Athena, once again in disguise.

Much encouraged, Odysseus challenged anyone to beat him in any contest. Only the great Philoctetes could beat him in archery and his javelin throwing was also very good. Perhaps in running, though, might someone outdistance him.

The king answered him, understanding his anger at the insult he had been given. But he preferred Odysseus to remember the Phaeacians for the things they really excelled in, which were music, dancing and feasting. So he called out the dancers and soon Odysseus was lost in admiration at the artistry of the young people before him. As they danced, the minstrel sung a song of the illicit love of Ares and Aphrodite. Apollo had seen them and reported them to Hephaestus, husband of the goddess of love. Hephaestus wove a golden net, strong and invisible and hung it over his marriage bed, before pretending to leave for Lemnos.

The minstrel continued with his song. Ares and Aphrodite lay down together and Hephaestus let down the net. He called to his fellow gods to be his witness and Hermes, Poseidon and Apollo answered his summons. At the sight of the two struggling in the net, Hermes and Apollo burst into laughter. Only Poseidon was not amused and urged Hephaestus to let Ares go. If the god of War did not make reparation, then

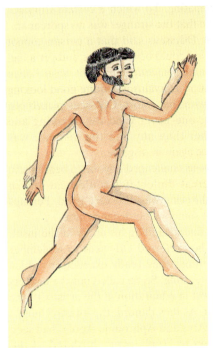

Poseidon himself would pay this debt. Hephaestus released them and Aphrodite fled to Cyprus and Ares to Thrace.

When the minstrel's song drew to a close, the king's son, Laodamus, danced with a partner and a ball, throwing it as they moved in time to a rhythm beaten out by those standing around. Odysseus was so impressed that he delighted Alcinous

Alcinous entertained Odysseus with sporting contests

with his praise. The happy king called on each of his chiefs to present their guest with a tunic, cloak and a talent of gold and ordered Euryalus to apologise for his insulting words. In obedience to his king, Euryalus presented Odysseus with a beautiful sword, which was accepted with grace.

When all the gifts were gathered and taken to the palace, the king asked his wife to bring a chest together with her own presents of clothes and to prepare hot water and a meal for their guest. When Odysseus was bathed and dressed, he met Nausicaa, who hoped that he would remember her, when he reached his home. Odysseus told her that he would always remember the one who had saved his life.

The meal began and Demedocus took up his lyre once more, singing of the famous Odysseus and his companions, who had entered Troy in a wooden horse. He sang of how the Greeks ran through the streets of the city, destroying and killing and he told of Odysseus himself, who with Menelaus sought out Deiphobus and put him to death.

Odysseus wept once more for his dead companions and Alcinous, seeing him, asked the minstrel to cease, for their guest was sorrowful. Then the king turned to Odysseus and begged to know his name and where he came from and what it was that made him weep when he heard tales of Troy.

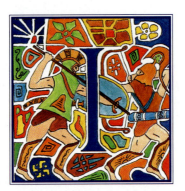

BOOK 9

"I am the son of Laertes, Odysseus. All people talk
of my skills, my glory has reached the heavens
and I live in merry, far away Ithaca,
where stands Mount Neriton, high and wooded.
All around and close to each other are islands,
Zakinthos with its many trees, Sami and Dulichi.
Under them all, Ithaca stands low on the open sea to the west;
the others all face the rising sun.
A stony place, but a famous birthplace of strong men.
I have not seen a sweeter place
than mine in the whole world."

So Odysseus introduced himself, before going on to tell of the
perils he faced when journeying back from Troy. The wind had
blown him first to Ismarus, he said, which he and his men
looted. When they had shared out the spoils, his companions,
relishing the wine and roasting the local meat, refused to
leave. They were set upon and lost many men before reaching
their ships and sailing away.

On route for Kithera, a storm blew them off course and after nine days they reached land, the home of the lotus eaters. There they found fresh water and some of the crew were sent to see what sort of people inhabited the land. But the men were fed with the fruit of the lotus and immediately forgot their home. They had to be brought back to the ship under duress and restrained there, weeping as they left.

On they sailed, a fleet of twelve ships, until they reached land once more. It was the home of rough, cave dwelling people, the Cyclopes. Odysseus and his men put ashore on an island nearby, a lush, green island, pasture for many goats. The men let fly their arrows at the animals and feasted on them until sunset.

The next day, said Odysseus, he left most of his companions on the island, taking only his ship and its crew to see what sort of people the Cyclopes were. As the ship neared the shore, Odysseus saw a cave, home of a giant, on a high point of land, surrounded by sheep pens. Leaving some men to guard the ship, he took twelve others with him, along with wine and provisions, to see what manner of man it was who lived there.

When they reached the cavern, no-one was there, only baskets full of cheeses hung from the roof and outside were young lambs and kids, penned separately. The men wanted to take some of the cheese back to the ship and then return for the animals before sailing off to join their companions. Odysseus, however, wanted to stay and see the giant. So they waited in the cave.

When the huge man returned, he drove his sheep before him, closed the mouth of the cave with a great rock and sat down to milk his flock. He lit a fire and by the light of the flames he saw Odysseus and his men. His great voice, when he asked them who they were, filled them with terror, but Odysseus explained that the winds had driven them to his land.

The giant said nothing, only picked up two men, dashed them to death on the floor, ate them and fell asleep. Trapped in the cave with the monster, Odysseus and his comrades lay all night, sleepless with horror.

At dawn the Cyclops ate two more men for his breakfast before leaving the cave with his flocks, not forgetting to replace the great rock as he went. Odysseus spent the day preparing a hefty olive branch which he found in the cave. Smoothed, sharpened, hardened in the fire, it made a formidable weapon.

Two more men were eaten by the Cyclops for his supper. When he had finished, Odysseus offered him some of the wine they had brought with them. When he had tasted the heady liquid, the giant asked for more and also asked Odysseus what his name was. Odysseus handed him another draught of wine

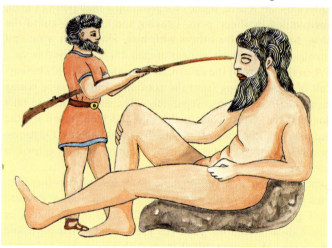

Odysseus put out the eye of Polyphemus

and said he was Nobody. In return for the wine, the Cyclops said, he would kill Nobody last. Then, unused to alcohol, he fell into a deep sleep.

Odysseus seized his chance. He held the point of his home made weapon in the fire and he and his companions burned out the one eye of the Cyclops while the giant slept. His roar of pain brought his compatriots to the closed door of the cave.

"What is wrong with you, Polyphemus, that you roar in the immortal night and cause us to lose sleep?

Polyphemus could only reply that Nobody had harmed him. So the other Cyclopes returned to their beds, assuming that he had had a nightmare. The rest of the night Odysseus spent lashing himself and his men to the undersides of the sheep. In the morning, Polyphemus let the animals out of the cave, stroking the back of the woolly fleece of each one as it passed him, to make sure it was a sheep and not one of his enemies.

In this way, Odysseus and the remainder of his men escaped, reached their ship and put to sea. But Odysseus could not resist taunting Polyphemus and the angry giant hurled a great rock at them. His men begged him to stop, but their captain continued,

'Oh Cyclops, if any mortal in the world asks you, to learn of the incurable blindness of your eye, tell them it was done by that warrior Odysseus, son of Laertes, from the island of Ithaca.'

The Cyclops offered up a prayer to Poseidon, god of the sea. He begged that Odysseus might never reach home, but if he was destined to do so, the giant prayed that he would be delayed and find things faring badly when he did reach his home. Poseidon paid attention to his prayer.

BOOK 10

Odysseus continued with his story. He and his men reached the kingdom of Aeolus, Guardian of the Winds. It was a rich land and they stayed for a while, entertaining the king with the story of the war with Troy. When they came to leave, Aeolus presented Odysseus with a leather bag in which, tightly secured, were all four winds. He gave them a gentle breeze to set them on their way and soon they were in sight of Ithaca. An exhausted Odysseus fell asleep and his men, thinking there was gold in the leather bag, opened it and out rushed the winds. In no time at all, Ithaca had disappeared from sight and the ship was blown back to Aeolia.

The king, realising that the gods were against Odysseus, refused to help him again and they continued on their voyage, this time with no wind to help them on their way. They rowed for many days until they reached the land of the Laestrygonians. Most of the fleet put in to harbour, but Odysseus tied his ship up in a nearby cove. When the Laestrygonians pelted the ships with rocks and harpooned the men, carrying them away to eat, Odysseus cut his ship loose and he and his crew were the only ones to escape.

On they sailed, said Odysseus, until they put ashore on the island of Aeaea, home of the sorceress, Circe. There he sent a scouting party ahead to Circe's home, under the command of Eurylochus. The goddess invited them in, but a suspicious Eurylochus stayed outside. Circe drugged them and turned them into wild pigs.

When Eurylochus had waited for his men in vain for some time, he returned to report them missing to Odysseus, who decided to go and look for himself. On his way to Circe's home, he met Hermes, who told him what had happened to his men and gave him some advice along with a plant, an antidote to her spells.

An amazed Circe, on entertaining Odysseus and discovering that the powerful potion she had slipped into his wine had no effect, asked him who he was. She was sure, she said, that he must be the great Odysseus and he, in turn, extracted a promise from her that she would do him no harm, before the two lay together. Then Odysseus was bathed, clothed and a feast was laid out for

Circe changed the crew into pigs

him, but he could not eat, he said, while his companions were not free.

Whereupon Circe went to the pigsty and released the men from their spell, making each more handsome than he had been before. As they rejoiced and settled down to eat, Circe suggested that Odysseus go to his ship, haul it ashore and bring the rest of his men to her house. Doing her bidding, Odysseus found his men relieved that he was not dead and only Eurylochus did not want to join the banquet, sure that it was a trick to prevent them leaving. It was suggested that, as he did not want to go, he stay and guard the ship, but in the end, he accompanied them to Circe's house. There the exhausted sailors ate and drank their fill. They stayed for a year. At last, the men begged Odysseus to take them home.

So Odysseus asked Circe to allow them to leave, but she said that before she could send him home, he had to visit Hades, in his Underworld kingdom and seek the counsel of Teiresias, a blind seer. The North Wind, said Circe, would blow him to a beach which was surrounded by the bushy woodlands of Persephone. There he would beach his boat and strike inland. Where the burning waters met the river Styx, he must dig a trench, into which he must pour honey, milk, wine and barley, an offering to the dead. When he had made an animal sacrifice, the souls of the dead would rise. Odysseus was not to contact any of them, and had to keep them away from the sacrificial blood, before he saw Teiresias, who would give him the directions for home.

At daybreak, Odysseus sought out his men, but one of them, Elpenor, had got drunk in the night, missed his footing and died of a broken neck. Odysseus told his men that they were on their way again, but first they had to go to Hades. So it was not with joy in their hearts but in dread of that place that they launched their vessel once more on the seas.

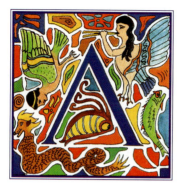

BOOK 11

With heavy hearts but a good wind in their sails, continued Odysseus, they followed Circe's instructions and came to the place she had described, by the Styx. There he dug the trench and poured in the milk and honey, wine and barley. After praying he cut the throats of two sheep and out of the ground came the spirits of the dead.

The first to arrive was the last to descend, Elpenor, who, in their hurry to depart, they had not buried. He begged Odysseus to give him a proper funeral before he returning to Ithaca, so that his soul could rest in peace and this, said Odysseus, he promised.

The next soul to rise from Hades was the spirit of Anticleia, mother of Odysseus, who had still been alive when he left for the Trojan War. But Odysseus could not speak with her until the seer arrived. At last, the spirit of Teiresias rose and drank blood from the sacrificed sheep before he prophecied.

Odysseus, said Teiresias, would have a difficult journey, for Poseidon, god of the sea, was against him. He and his crew would reach home, he foretold if, when they passed the island of Thrinacie, they did not touch the sheep of Apollo which grazed there. If any of the animals came to harm, then Odysseus would lose his ship and his men and there would be trouble waiting for him at home. He would arrive late, to find his palace full of people feasting and wasting his possessions. He had to put these to death and then set out once more, this time holding an oar, until he reached a people who never salted their food and knew nothing of the sea. When someone asked him about the winnowing fan he held, then he had to sacrifice to Poseidon before returning home. In the end, said Teiresias, his death would be gentle.

After listening to the prophecy, Odysseus was told that he

Agamemnon is murdered

could speak to any of the spirits if they had first drunk of the sacrificial blood and, in this way, he was able to talk to his mother. She told him that his son was well but his father grieved for him, wearing rags and sleeping out of doors. She herself had died of a broken heart, waiting for his return.

Then Odysseus listed, for King Alcinous and Queen Arete, all the souls he had met, rising from Hades, among them Alcmene, mother of Heracles. Jocasta was there, the mother of Oedipus, along with Ariadne, who had helped Theseus escape from the labyrinth. Then wearied by his long tale, he asked to be allowed to sleep.

The people had sat spellbound as they listened to his story and the king begged for more. Reluctantly, Odysseus continued. The next soul he had met was that of Agamemnon, who told how he had died, along with all his men, at the hands of Aegisthus, at a banquet. And of how his wife, Clytaemnestra, had murdered Cassandra, his concubine. Never trust a woman, said Agamemnon, before asking, in vain, if Odysseus had news of Orestes, his son.

The soul of Achilles appeared, said Odysseus. He also wanted news of his son, Neoptolemus, and Odysseus was able to tell him of his daring feats against the Trojans and his bravery when they finally took Troy.

Ajax, still bitter because Odysseus had won the armour of Achilles, refused to speak to him. Minos was there, and Orion, said Odysseus, along with Tantalus, who stood near a pool, unable to drink from it when his thirst drove him mad and unable to reach the fruit which grew above his head.

Then, said Odysseus, the dead gathered round him in their thousands, the sound of their voices filling him with dread and he ran for his ship before he could be dragged down to Hades with them.

BOOK 12

Odysseus persevered with his story. They returned, he said, to Aeaea, for the purpose of burying Elpenor. When they had finished and built the barrow, Circe appeared, with food and wine. Bad luck, she told Odysseus, that he had gone down alive into Hades. While every one else had only had one death, he would have two. And she persuaded the men to rest and eat, to be ready to leave at dawn the next day, but took Odysseus to one side, asking for an account of what had happened.

Circe told him what would occur when they left her island. They would meet the Sirens. The sound of their song would cast a spell on them so strong that they would never reach home. They were to plug their ears and sail by. If Odysseus wanted to hear their lovely music, he would first have to tie himself to the mast, to resist their magic.

Then they would have the choice of two directions. One would lead them to a rocky place so dangerous that even birds were unable to fly by in safety and no ship had ever escaped the terrible breakers, with the exception of the Argo, captained by

Jason, who had been helped by the goddess Hera. The other way led between two great rocks and the Scylla lived in the tallest. This was a female monster, twelve feet long, with six dog like heads on the end of six long necks, their mouths armed with gruesome teeth. Near the lower rock, the terrible Charybdis sucked the water down deep before blowing it back in a great surge three times a day. Circe warned Odysseus to keep nearer to Scylla's rock and drive his ship through fast. If he negotiated the way between the rocks in safety, he would then reach Thrinacie, where Apollo kept his sheep. Circe reiterated the warning of Teiresias, saying that if any of the animals were harmed, then his ship and crew would be destroyed.

At sun rise, continued Odysseus, they left Circe's island and he related her prophecies to the men, warning them of the Sirens and telling them not to undo him, if he tied himself to the mast. As they neared the island where the Sirens lived, he gave his

Odysseus tied to the mast

crew softened wax to put in their ears and had himself lashed to the mast. The wind dropped and all that could be heard was the soft swish of oars until Odysseus heard the beautiful, beguiling song. He begged his men to set him free, but they had been warned. They rowed vigoruously and at last the song died away.

The sea turned rough as they neared the rocks where the Scylla lived. Odysseus related how he told his men to row hard and to keep as near to the cliff as they could. Through the straits they rowed in terror, while on one side Charybdis sucked the sea down with a great roar and spewed it up again and on the other side the six long necks of the Scylla reached out and the heads with their great teeth snatched six of the crew and ate them as they struggled.

When they reached Apollo's island, Odysseus reminded the men again of the warnings of Teiresias and Circe, not to harm any of the sheep which grazed there. He suggested they rowed past, but the men, led by Eurylochus, promised not to touch the animals if only they could anchor in the bay, land on the pleasant shore and eat from the provisions on board.

That done, they settled down for the night, but a gale blew up and they had to beach the ship and drag it into a cave. For a month the wind blew so strongly that they were unable to leave. When their provisions were gone, the hungry men fished and hunted for game. But Eurylochus had a plan. While Odysseus was praying for help to the gods, he and his fellows rounded up Apollo's sheep and killed them, offering the sacrifice to the gods before eating the succulent meat. A horrified Odysseus had no way of making amends. The deed was done and the crew feasted off the meat for six days.

On the seventh day, said Odysseus, the wind dropped and they put to sea once more. But suddenly a dreadful storm sprang up. The ship was struck by lightning, the crew thrown overboard and he himself, clinging to some of the ship's timber, found himself back near Scylla's rock. Somehow he escaped the clutches of both monsters and drifted for nine days until he was washed ashore on Calypso's island, Ogygia.

BOOK 13

At last Odysseus had come to an end of his story and was allowed to sleep. As the sun rose the following day, King Alcinous himself stored the gift of a tripod and cauldron on the ship he was providing, along with the chest full of clothes and gold. Odysseus, impatient to be off, thanked the Phaeacian people and prayed for happiness and health for all. A libation was poured to the gods, Odysseus took his leave of the king and queen and went down to the sea and his ship, where he fell into an exhausted sleep.

While Odyssesus still slumbered, the ship was beached in the cove of Phorcys, on Ithaca. The Phaeacians laid the unconscious warrior on the sand, along with his gifts, before setting back to their own land. The watching Poseidon was angry. Although he had not said Odysseus would never return, he had not expected to see him reach his own land with gifts of gold and rich materials. In his anger he took it out on the returning Phaeacians, anchoring their ship to the sea bed before it could enter harbour. King Alcinous recognized the hand of Poseidon and made sacrifice to him.

At the very same moment, on Ithaca, Odysseus woke. But he had been away so long, he did not know his own land. He thought he had been purposely set down in some isolated spot and was surprised to find all his gifts intact. Then Athena appeared to him, this time disguised as a shepherd and it was she who told him he had reached Ithaca. A suspicious Odysseus, always prepared for a trick, wove a long tale to explain his presence on the island, before the goddess revealed herself to him. Odysseus kissed the ground and prayed that he

might see his son grow to be a man.

Instructed by Athena, Odysseus hid his riches in a cave. The two sat down and planned a way to rid his palace of the suitors. The goddess vowed to change his appearance, making him look very old. No-one, she said, not even his wife, would know him. He must go to the man who

Athena reveals herself to Odysseus

looked after the pigs and get news from him, regarding the suitors, while Athena went to Sparta to bring Telemachus safely home.

Athena put out her wand and touched Odysseus. His skin wrinkled, his limbs shrank and he lost his hair. His eyes grew dim and his clothes became rags. A stout stick appeared in his hand and the goddess finished his disguise by putting a pack on his back.

BOOK 14

Odysseus found Eumaeus, the swineherd, making sandals for himself. His many pigs were guarded by fierce dogs, which would have attacked the hero had the swineherd not thrown stones at them and sent them away. Eumaeus apologised for his humble home, as he invited Odysseus in for a meal. His old master, he said, who was very wealthy, had cared for him better than his new ones. He killed a piglet and roasted it over the fire, serving a bowl of wine as they ate. The best meat, he said, was eaten by the suitors, who feasted night and day, drinking the most excellent wine as well. They must have heard that his old master was dead, to behave in that way.

Odysseus asked the name of his old master. Perhaps, as he had travelled far and wide, he could give Eumaeus news of him. Eumaeus said that many beggars came to Ithaca, saying they had news, hoping for reward, and Penelope would listen to their tales, weeping. Perhaps his ragged guest was hoping for some new clothes in return for a tale. But he himself believed Odysseus was dead.

Odysseus swore to him that his master would return that very month. Eumaeus did not believe him, only wished it could be so. Even Telemachus, son of Odysseus, was a disappointment, he said, for he had gone to look for news of his father and now the suitors were waiting to kill him when he returned. Then the swineherd asked who Odysseus was and where he had come from.

Odysseus and the Egyptian king

So Odysseus wove another tale. He was from Crete, he said, a man who loved ships and fighting. When the war with Troy began, he was asked to command a fleet and for nine years they fought the Trojans. When the city fell, he returned home, but after a month he embarked for Egypt. When they reached the Nile his men plundered and looted the farms and the Egyptians slew many and took the rest as slaves. As for himself, said Odysseus, he begged for mercy from the Egyptian king. It was granted and he spent seven years in that land before joining an expedition, arranged by a rogue, to Phoenicia. After two years there, he was put on a ship to Libya, but the vessel was wrecked in bad weather. All hands were lost, but he had managed to hold on to the mast. For nine days he was tossed by the waves until he landed, exhausted, on Thesprotia.

There, he was cared for and heard news of Odysseus. The Thesprotian king told him that Odysseus had accumulated much wealth. He had gone to ask the oracle of Zeus how he should return to his homeland and if he should go in disguise. A ship was waiting to take him. Odysseus told Eumaeus that he himself was put on another ship, bound for Dulichi, by the Thesprotians but the crew stripped him and robbed him when they were in sight of Ithaca. He had escaped and swum ashore. Eumaeus said he could accept the story except for the ridiculous part about Odysseus. He had heard from a man from Aetolia that Odysseus had been seen in Crete with Idomenus, repairing his damaged ships. No, he would not listen to lies.

The men who worked under Eumaeus arrived, driving their animals into the pens for the night. They feasted together on roast pig, bread and wine and Odysseus decided to test the character of Eumaeus. He told a story to the company gathered around the fire. It was at Troy, he said, that he was part of an attack led by Odysseus and Menelaus. When they reached the city walls, night fell and they lay down to sleep, each soldier wrapped in his thick cloak. But he had forgotten his. In the middle of the frosty night, he woke Odysseus, saying that he was dying from the cold and could not survive until morning. Odysseus told him to be quiet and then woke the others. The gods had sent him a dream, he announced. He needed a message taken to Agamemnon, asking for reinforcements. Immediately the gallant Thoas threw off his cloak and ran for the ships.

Eumaeus took the hint. He spread out skins for his ragged guest to sleep on and covered him with a thick blanket. Odysseus was happy to see that he was a careful man, who looked after his master's goods, for Eumaeus did not sleep by the fire, but took his sword and, wrapped in his cloak, left the hut to guard the pigs for the night.

BOOK 15

With Menelaus in Sparta in the meantime, Telemachus spent a sleepless night. Athena appeared to him, urging him to leave for home at once, for Penelope's father and brothers were trying to persuade her to marry Eurymachus. She also warned him that he was in danger of being ambushed between Ithaca and Samos. He must avoid those parts. When he landed, he was to go at once to the swineherd and stay with him for a night, sending him the next morning to give Penelope news that her son was safely home.

Telemachus wanted to be gone at once, but Peisistratus, son of Nestor, thought he ought to wait until dawn before taking leave of the king. At sun rise Menelaus would not detain him, but insisted on serving him with a meal and presenting him with gifts and asking him to give his greetings to Nestor when they reached Pylos.

So the two young men mounted their chariot and drove until dark, staying the night with a friend and catching sight of Pylos as the next day dawned. There, Telemachus begged Peisistratus to leave him at his ship, in the harbour, for he was sure to be detained by the hospitable Nestor and preferred to be on his way. At the risk of his father's anger, Peisistratus helped Telemachus aboard his vessel and said his goodbyes.

As Telemachus was making due sacrifice to the gods before leaving, a certain prophet, Theoclymenus, begged for sanctuary aboard the ship, for he had killed a man whose family was powerful and would put him to death. Telemachus agreed to take the man on board. They set sail for Ithaca with a good wind behind them.

At about the same time, Odysseus, still in the guise of a poor beggar, was eating with Eumaeus. He tested the swineherd again. He would go the next day, he said, to beg in the town, rather than outstay his welcome. He asked for advice and a guide. He would see the queen and tell her his story and perhaps the suitors would feed him and give him some work.

Eumaeus thought that was a dangerous idea. His guest would be courting death. It was safer to stay with him, for he was no trouble. If Telemachus arrived, he would be in a better position than they were, to offer a new set of clothes.

Odysseus thanked him and begged for news of Odysseus' parents. Laertes, father of Odysseus, was alive, said Eumaeus, but grieving pitifully not only for his son but also for his wife, who pined away when their son never returned from Troy. Eumaeus said he himself had always asked after her, when she was alive, for it was she who had raised him and educated him with her daughter, Ktimene. When Ktimene was married, he had been sent to the farm.

Odysseus asked Eumaeus how he had come to be a slave in Ithaca, far from home. Had he been stolen from his parents? And the swineherd answered him. His father had been king of the island of Syrie and his nurse was a Phoenician woman. When a ship came into harbour one day, from Phoenicia, one

Telemachus set sail for Ithaca

of the crew seduced the nurse. He discovered that she had been carried off by pirates as a young girl, but her parents had been wealthy. Scenting a reward, the sailor promised to take her back to her homeland, but the nurse had more to offer. When they were ready to depart, she would steal not only gold for them, but also the king's son, who would fetch a good price on the market.

That was how Eumaeus came to be so far from home, for the nurse was as good as her word But she fell overboard during the voyage and bad weather swept the ship to Ithaca, where King Laertes bought the child for a good price.

His story finished, Eumaeus and Odysseus settled down for what was left of the night while, further up the coast, Telemachus quietly dropped anchor and rowed into land. Telling his crew to take the ship on to the harbour, he said he had to go and see the swineherd. He would be with them later, when he would pay them for the journey. Theoclymenus asked where he should go and Telemachus advised him to seek out Eurymachus, who was the best of the suitors. As he uttered the words, a hawk appeared, holding a dove in its claws and Theoclymenus saw it as a good omen.

The ship sailed for the town and Telemachus took up his spear and set out alone for Eumaeus and his farms.

BOOK 16

Eumaeus, preparing breakfast with Odysseus, was overjoyed to see Telemachus and as the three sat down to eat, the boy asked who the ragged guest might be. The swineherd explained that he was a man from Crete and asked Telemachus to receive him into his house. Telemachus said he would fit the man out with new clothes and a weapon, but could not allow him near the palace and the suitors, for they were a rough crowd and no-one could fight alone against so many.

Odysseus asked how it was that these men behaved so badly and yet the people of Ithaca did nothing. Telemachus tried to explain that the people, though apathetic, were not against him. The trouble was that his mother would neither refuse the men nor marry one of them. Then he asked Eumaeus to go to the palace and let his mother know that he had returned safely.

The swineherd gone, Athena came to the door of the hut, visible only to Odysseus. She beckoned him outside, where she returned him to his normal self. Telemachus was astonished to see the change and took Odysseus for a god. He could not believe it was his father, but when at last he understood that Odysseus had returned, he wept as the two embraced.

When Odysseus asked for the names of the suitors and made known his wish to destroy them, Telemachus was horrified. There were far too many of them. Who would be on the side of Odysseus? His father said Athena and Zeus should be more than sufficient allies. He proposed going into the town disguised as a be-

ggar, accompani-
ed by Eumaeus.
Telemachus wo-
uld preceed him,
going into the
great hall where
the suitors were
and, at a sign, ga-
ther all the wea-
pons from the
walls, leaving two
swords, spears
and shields in a
place where he
and Odysseus co-
uld seize them at
the right mome-
nt. If anyone ask-
ed him why he
was taking the

*Telemachus thought
his father was a god*

weapons, he was to say he was taking them for cleaning, or some such excuse. He was to tell no-one that his father had returned, not even his mother.

While these plans were being laid, the ship that had carried Telemachus back put into port. The crew sent a messenger to announce the return of Telemachus. The suitors, who thought they had dealt with him, were not at all happy at the news. They went to the sea front, where they hauled up the ship which had failed to ambush the returning youth. Some wanted to lie in wait for him on the road into town but Amphinomus preferred to learn the wishes of the gods before they did anything they regretted. With that, they returned to the palace and the great hall.

Eumaeus had delivered his message to Penelope, who had learned of the plans to murder Telemachus. She summoned up her courage and faced the suitors, addressing Antinous, accusing him of plotting the death of her son. Eurymachus soothed her, promising that no harm would come to Telemachus.

While these events were taking place in town, Eumaeus returned to his farm and Athena, not ready for him to recognize Odysseus, turned that hero back into a ragged beggar.

BOOK 17

Asking the swineherd to bring along their guest later, to do his begging in town, Telemachus set off at dawn for his father's house. His nurse, Eurycleia, wept with pleasure at the sight of him and soon he was reunited with his mother. She wanted to hear all his news, but he only told her the information he had received from Menelaus, that Odysseus was a prisoner of Calypso. The seer Theoclymenus interrupted and told the queen that the news was wrong. Odysseus, according to his interpretations of signs and omens, was in Ithaca at that very moment.

Also at that moment Odysseus and Eumaeus were approaching the town. They met a certain Melantheus, who scorned Odysseus for his ragged clothes, laughing at the idea of the suitors throwing things at him as he begged in the palace. Somehow Odysseus restrained himself and Eumaeus told Melantheus that if Odysseus had been there, he would have dealt with him sharply. There was little chance of Odysseus returning, retorted Melentheus before he made his way to the palace and took his place at supper alongside the suitors.

Outside the town, Eumaeus and his ragged companion paused. On the ground lay a dog, thin and mangy. On seeing Odysseus, it wagged its tail but it was too weak to get up. Wiping away a tear before he spoke, Odysseus drew the animal to the attention of Eumaeus, who said it had once belonged to Odysseus. It had been a sleek and active dog, he said, but now it was grieving for its master. As Eumaeus went into the great hall of the palace, taking a seat at supper near Telemachus, the dog died.

Odysseus entered the hall and sat on the floor beside the door.

Telemachus sent Eumaeus over to him with a bowl of food and a message suggesting that he went around the suitors and begged. When he did so, most of them gave him food and asked who he was. Melantheus answered them, saying that he only knew that the beggar had come with the swineherd. Anti-

*Odysseus
and his dog*

nous asked Eumaeus why he had brought a stranger into town to pester them. Telemachus settled the argument that followed but, when Odysseus approached Antinous with his begging bowl, he was refused. Odysseus accused him of being mean, saying,

> 'Alas, you don't have brains to match your looks.
> You wouldn't give a poor man salt from your own home,
>   you who sit at a stranger's table
> and cannot bear to treat me to a mouthful of bread,
>   when there is plenty.'

Antinous snatched up a stool and threw it, striking Odysseus in the back, but it had no effect. Odysseus resumed his seat by the door while many of the suitors were concerned, feeling that Antinous had gone too far. Telemachus had difficulty controlling himself and later, when the affair came to the ears of Penelope, she asked for the stranger to be brought before her, sending Eumaeus with the request.

Odysseus told Eumaeus that he would wait until sunset, for he was worried by the suitors, having been struck by one of them. He would be safer to go to the queen after dark.

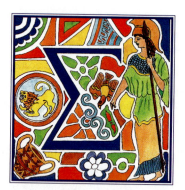

BOOK 18

As Odysseus sat by the door, he was approached by a resident beggar, one Irus, a large and greedy man, who told him to be off. Odysseus said there was room for both of them but, if the man continued to speak to him in that way, old as he looked he would get the better of him in a fight. In no time, to the delight of the watching suitors, the two beggars had challenged each other to a boxing match. The winner, said Antinous, would be given a whole joint of roasted goat.

When Odysseus hitched up his rags and prepared himself to fight, revealing his great stature, Irus took fright but was dragged into the ring, where Odysseus easily beat him, to the joy of those watching, who were glad to be rid of him. Antinous presented Odysseus with the goat and Amphinomus sat next to him, toasting him with wine, wishing him health and happiness. Odysseus tried, but in vain, to warn his new companion, suggesting that he return home, for he was sure that King Odysseus would be back soon and would have no mercy on the suitors.

Meanwhile, the queen, Penelope, decided to pay a visit to the suitors. While waiting for her attendants to prepare her, she fell into a deep sleep, when Athena made her look younger and more beautiful. When she woke and entered the great hall, all were filled with desire for her. She spoke to Telemachus, accusing him of allowing a stranger to be insulted in her house, but Telemachus explained that, although he was quite unable, on his own, to take on the suitors, Odysseus had beaten Irus in a fight. Then Eurymachus praised Penelope for her beauty, but she replied that she had lost her looks and zest for life when her husband, Odysseus, had left for Troy and not returned. She recalled how Odysseus had left his parents and his estates in her care, telling her that not all soldiers returned from battle and to marry again when their son became a man. Soon she would have to do as he had wished, but surely, said Penelope, men brought gifts to their ladies and their own food to the banquets they arranged. With that, each suitor presented Penelope with a handsome gift before she retired and they continued with their revels.

As night fell, three fires were lit to give light and Odysseus took the place of the

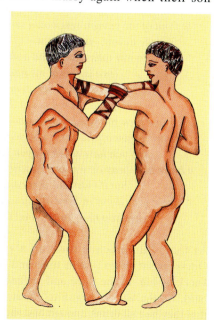

A boxing match

maids who attended to the flames. Eurymachus scoffed at his
bald head shining in the blaze and offered him a job on one of
his farms. Odysseus answered,

> 'If only the two of us could compete in work,
> in the spring when the days are long,
> to harvest the abundant grass, each
> with a curved sickle in hand,
> to show our worth until evening,
> without eating a mouthful.
> Or to drive cattle, shouting, the best cattle, fair, well fed,
> matched in age and of the same strength,
> an untameable pair and the earth in the furrows falling
> in front of the plough; you would see how straight I would
> cut the furrow. And if the son of Cronos roused us
> to war today and I had a shield to hold,
> two lances in my hand and
> a bronze helmet on my head,
> you would see me run to the front line
> and then you would swear what a glutton I was.
> However you offend easily and your heart is unfeeling
> and you have taken it upon yourself to be
> a brave hero because you are associated with some wastrels.
> But if Odysseus ever came home,
> these wide doors in front of you would be too narrow
> when you rush for the road in your haste.'

At that, Eurymachus took up a stool and threw it but
Odysseus sat down just in time and the stool hit a servant,
knocking him to the floor and spilling the pitcher of wine he
held. As the suitors began to shout, Telemachus suggested
that they had all drunk enough and should retire for the night.

BOOK 19

Odysseus sought out his son. It was time to put the first part of his plan into motion. Telemachus ordered Eurycleia, his nurse, to keep the women away while they removed the weapons from the walls of the great hall, explaining that the smoke from the fires had tarnished them. Once all helmets, swords and spears were locked away, Telemachus retired for the night.

In the hall, Odysseus was joined by Penelope. They sat by the fireside and Penelope asked Odysseus who he was and where he came from, hoping for news of her husband. Odysseus begged her to ask anything of him, but not to enquire of his ancestry, for it would be most upsetting for him.

Penelope explained how her husband had joined the fleet for Troy and not returned. She said that rulers from all around had come to ask for her hand and would not return to their estates until she had chosen one of them. She had begun work on her loom, saying that she would make the decision when the weaving was finished and every night, for three years, she undid the day's work. But they had discovered her ploy and now she had to finish the cloth. Then Penelope begged once more for Odysseus to tell her about himself. So Odysseus again found himself telling a false tale.

*'In the midst of a turbid sea lies the island of Krete,
beautiful and lush. Closed in by the ocean it boasts myriad
inhabitants and ninety towns.
Every race of people has its own language.
Most are Achaeans, then there are the lion-hearted Kretans,
the worthy Kydonians, three tribes of Dorians and the generous
Pelasgians. The greatest city is Knossos, where Minos,
an aquaintance of Zeus, reigned for nine years.
He was father of my father Deucalion who bore two sons,
myself, who am named Aithona,
and the commander Idomeneus who went to Troy
with the two sons of Atreus in their curved ships.'*

It was himself, Aithona, continued Odysseus, who had welcomed Penelope's husband to Krete when his ship had been driven off course while heading for Troy. The weather kept Odysseus on the island for twelve days, but he resumed his journey on the thirteenth.

Penelope wept as she heard news of her husband, but decided to test the story teller. She asked him to describe the clothes Odysseus was wearing and to depict one of the crew. Odysseus painted a picture of a man in a purple cloak, describing the brooch which fastened it, along with the wonderfully woven tunic he wore. He spoke of his companion, Eurybates and Penelope welcomed him as an honoured guest when she heard the correct account, for she herself had made the clothes Odysseus described.

As Penelope's tears flowed, Odysseus begged her to stop. He had news of her husband's return, he said. He was close by, on his way home with a great fortune. Penelope found it difficult to believe his words and called her maids to wash his feet and prepare a bed for him. Odysseus declined and said he was used to sleeping on the floor, but Penelope insisted that Eurycleia bathe his feet.

Odysseus was worried that his old nurse would recognize a scar if she washed him and recalled to himself how he had received it while hunting as a young boy, many years before.

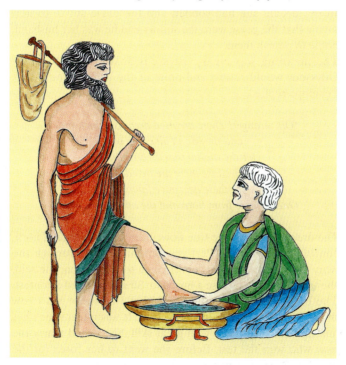

Odysseus has his feet washed

He had been right to worry, for as Eurycleia took hold of his foot she saw the scar and knew Odysseus at once, crying out in her delight. Athena made sure that Penelope did not hear the woman's exclamations as Odysseus ordered his nurse not to reveal his presence to anyone.

His feet cleaned and rubbed with oil, Odysseus settled by the fire once more and Penelope asked him about a dream she had. She had seen an eagle swoop down and kill all her geese. In her dream she had sobbed and the eagle spoke to her, saying that the geese were the suitors and he was her husband, home to punish them.

The meaning was clear, Odysseus answered. Obviously Odysseus would return and none of the suitors would live. Penelope replied,

> 'Oh, stranger! There are mad dreams, which fade
> and they don't all come true
> for the mortal that dreams them.
> Because there are two doors
> for these deceptive fantasies.
> One is made from horn and the other from ivory.'

The dreams which came true flowed through the door of horn, continued the queen. Perhaps hers had come through the ivory door, whose dreams never came to pass. Soon, she said, she would have to choose a husband. So she planned a contest. The bidders for her hand would have to shoot an arrow through a standing row of twelve axes. It was a feat which her husband could perform with great skill. She would marry the man who won the test. Before she went to her room for the night, Odysseus urged her to hold the contest as soon as possible.

BOOK 20

Odysseus tossed and turned on his bed of skins. As he lay pondering the problem of how he could take on the suitors single handed, Athena came to him. Had she not always watched over him, she asked? He should have more trust in her powers, she said, as she put him to sleep.

As Odysseus slept, Penelope lay awake, praying to Artemis and longing for sleep or even death.

'Even a sorrowful person, who is given a burden of grief and beats his breast all day long, when night falls, he sleeps. Because when his eyelids droop, good and bad are buried in a state of oblivion. But fate sends me bad dreams. This very night he was at my side once more, as he was when he went to war, and I was so full of happinesss when he really spoke and it didn't seem like the dream it was.'

The new day dawned and Odysseus woke to hear Penelope weeping. He rose and prayed to Zeus for some sign that the gods would be with him and a great roll of thunder roared from the sky in response. The palace came to life, servants

rekindled the fires and Eurycleia set the maids to work, cleaning, for it was a public holiday.

Eumaeus joined Odysseus in the courtyard and they were in turn joined by the goat herd, Philoetius, who welcomed Odysseus, noting his ragged appearance and saying how cruel the gods were sometimes and yet something in the stranger, he said, reminded him of Odysseus. He still lived in hope, he said, that his old master would return one day.

The suitors, meanwhile, had been discussing between themselves ways and means of ridding themselves of Telemachus, when an eagle soared above them, a dove in its claws. It was a sign, said the seer Amphinomus, that their

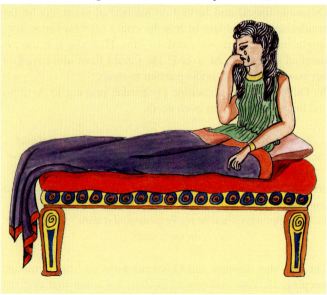

Penelope longs for sleep

plans would not succeed. So they all went to the palace to eat, where Telemachus himself served Odysseus from the table, ordering the suitors to leave him alone.

A certain Ctesippus picked up the hoof of a cow and hurled it at Odysseus. The missile missed its mark and Telemachus sprang to his feet. If the hoof had hit his guest, he said, he would have drawn his sword and killed Ctesippus. If he had to put up with the suitors, at least they could behave themselves in his house. If they were out to murder him, then he would prefer death to watching them mistreat his guests and his servants.

The next to speak was Agelaus. Let Telemachus, he said, go to his mother and tell her to choose a husband, for it was quite plain that Odysseus would not return. Telemachus replied that he had urged his mother to make the choice, but more than that he could not do. The suitors roared with laughter at that. They laughed until they cried and then Theoclymenus called out with a warning,

'Oh unhappy men! What calamity lies in wait for you? Darkness circles your heads, your faces, your limbs. You break out in lamentation. There, on your cheeks the tears run. The lovely walls drip with blood. The hall and courtyard are filled with the shades of the dead, who run around in sunless gloom. The sun is lost to us and confusion reigns.'

The suitors laughed and taunted the seer, who reiterated his warning as he left the palace. The men turned their attentions to Telemachus, teasing him in turn, but he kept quiet, only watching for a sign from Odysseus.

BOOK 21

Penelope made her way to the store room. There lay the great bow which had been given to Odysseus many years before. In tears as she took up the heavy weapon with its quiver of arrows, she made her way with the bow to the great hall and addressed the men who were paying her court. Whoever could string the bow, she said, and shoot an arrow through each of twelve axes, would be her husband.

Telemachus decided to try his hand at the task, only to see if he could string his father's bow, but after three futile attempts he gave up at a sign from Odysseus. Antinous then suggested that they should take turns, going around the table from left to right. With the exception of Antinous and Eurymachus, who held back, one after the other attempted to string the bow but failed. Meanwhile, Odysseus followed Eumaeus and Philoetius into the courtyard, asking them whose side they would be on if Odysseus came back. Reassured by their responses, he showed them his scar and they recognized him with joy.

Odysseus gave them instructions. They were to return to the hall and when the suitors refused to allow Odysseus to attempt to string the bow, Eumaeus was to hand it to him. The women were

to be locked into their rooms and Philoetius was given the task of securing the courtyard gate.

Back in the hall, Eurymachus warmed the wooden bow by the fire and flew into a rage when he failed to string it. Antinous suggested that a holiday was not the time for such things. They should drink some wine and in the morning, if the goatherd Melantheus would bring in the best animals, they would sacrifice to Apollo, the archer god, and only then test their skills.

The ragged Odysseus asked if he might try his hand. Fearful that he might succeed, Antinous protested loudly and Penelope accused him of bad manners. Eurymachus said that they didn't want people to say that a beggar could do what they had failed to achieve. Penelope said he should be allowed to try and Telemachus ordered her to her room, saying that it was his decision, as son of the house, to say who could be given the bow.

Eumaeus handed the weapon to Odysseus, Eurycleia was sent to lock the women into their rooms and Philoetius secured the great gate to the courtyard. As the suitors scoffed, Odysseus tested the bow, strung it and tried the string. The note sounded mellow and silence fell as he picked up an arrow. His shot passed through the twelve axes. Telemachus, at a sign from Odysseus, put on his sword and stood beside his father in the doorway.

Odysseus strings the great bow

BOOK 22

Odysseus took up an arrow and shot Antinous, the wound fatal. The suitors rose and turned to the walls, searching for weapons but there were none. As they accused the ragged stranger of killing a nobleman, assuming it was an accident, Odysseus spoke.

'Dogs, who thought I would not return to my homeland,
squandered my home with no feeling,
lay down with unwilling maids and, while I lived,
wanted my wife as your own without fear of the gods
who live in the skies or
that some day an avenger might come.'

Eurymachus said that if he was truly Odysseus, then his anger was just. However, the chief perpetrator of the deeds was Antinous and now he was dead. He asked that he and the others be spared. They would pay taxes to make up for the food and drink they had used and each bring gifts in reparation. But Odysseus refused. Eurymachus drew his sword and Odysseus let fly an arrow which killed him. Telemachus slew Amphinomous as he attacked Odysseus and then went to

Odysseus shoots Antinous

get the helmets, shields and spears that they had put aside earlier, enough to equip themselves, Eumaeus and Philoetius. As his supply of arrows dwindled, Odysseus put on his armour and took up his spear. But Melantheus slipped out of the hall and found the store room door unlocked. He found armour and weapons and brought them to the suitors. When he set out for more, he was discovered and tied to a pillar but Odysseus and his three companions were now faced and outnumbered by well armed and protected men.

Disguised as Mentor once more, Athena came to the rescue. With the goddess on their side, Odysseus and his companions slew the suitors one by one. The minstrel Phemius threw himself and his lyre at the feet of the king and Odysseus, at a word from Telemachus, allowed him to leave, along with the herald, for they were innocent of any crime. At last it was finished, and all those who had courted Penelope lay dead.

Eurycleia was summoned. Odysseus asked for all those servants, who had been disloyal in his absence, to be brought to the hall, where they were ordered to carry out the dead and clean the tables and chairs. Then they were put to death, along with Melantheus. Odysseus ordered Eurycleia to build a fire and bring him sulphur, which he threw on the flames to disinfect the palace. While he was doing this, the old nurse told her companions of their master's return and soon they gathered round Odysseus, weeping with joy as they embraced him.

BOOK 23

Eurycleia went to Penelope, crying out that Odysseus was home and had killed all the suitors. The queen would not believe her, but Eurycleia insisted that the ragged stranger was indeed her master and had slain Penelope's lovers almost single handed. The queen was still unable to believe the story and went to the hall where she sat by the fire and gazed at Odysseus, who was still dressed in rags and disguised as an old man. Still she did not recognize him and Telemachus accused her of having a heart of stone. Odysseus, understanding his wife's dilemma, turned to Telemachus. They had a problem, he said, for they had killed many noblemen. His son, his companio... ᵗ ᵗʰe servants should wash, dress, call the musician and make merry, so that the people outside would think the suitors were still there.

Odysseus himself bathed and dressed in his own clothes. Athena made him look even more handsome before he took his place once more beside Penelope, who, still sceptical, wanted to test him. She told Eurycleia to make up the big bed for him, outside his old bedroom. When he heard this, Odysseus asked how his bed had been moved, for he had made it himself and its manufacture was secret. The room had been built around an olive tree and he had used the trunk for the base of the bed. On hearing her husband say this, Penelope recognized him at last and in tears the two were reunited.

Then Odysseus told his wife that his troubles were not yet over. He told her how Teiresias, from Hades, had told him to

wander the land with an oar until he came to a race of people who did not know the sea and never used salt. There, when someone asked why he carried a winnowing bat, he had to plant the oar and make sacrifice to Poseidon. Then he could return home. Death, he said, would come gently in his old age.

Penelope recognises Odysseus

Before husband and wife slept, Odysseus recounted all his
adventures from the time he had left for Troy. And when
morning came he left his home and belongings once more in
Penelope's care as he went to see his father. He told her to
stay in her room and speak to no one, for soon all would know
that he had killed the suitors.

BOOK 24

Hermes gathered the souls of the suitors, taking them to the
asphodel fields where the spirits of the dead lived. There
Achilles, Patroclus and Agamemnon were gathered, discussing
the death and funeral of Achilles. They buried him, said
Agamemnon, on the Hellespont, where they built a great
mound which could be seen far out to sea. As they spoke,
Hermes arrives with the suitors and Agamemnon's soul
recognized that of Amphimedon. Amphimedon described for
Agamemnon how they had paid court to Penelope. He told of
her weaving at the loom and how she unpicked her work each
night. He told of the return of Odysseus, how he had strung
the great bow and how they had fallen to his deadly arrows.

Meanwhile, Odysseus had reached the cottage where his grieving father lived. He sent Telemachus to prepare a meal while he found his father alone in the vineyard, dressed in ragged and dirty working clothes, looking old, worn and unhappy. Odysseus, going up to him and not knowing what to say, remarked how the beautifully kept gardens compared unfavourably with his attire. Who was his master? Was he in Ithaca? He had met a man from Ithaca once, who said he was the son of Laertes. He had entertained him and given him many rich presents.

Yes, he was in Ithaca, the old man told Odysseus, but the land had been ruined by rogues. The man he had met was his son who was dead and he had not been able to bury his body and mourn for him properly. As the old man began to weep for his son, Odysseus could bear it no longer and embraced his father, telling him that he had returned and killed the suitors.

Laertes could not believe it and asked for proof. Odysseus showed him his scar and reminded him of a time when he was a small child and learned the names of the trees in the gardens. So happy was the father to know the son that he collapsed. When he recovered, Laertes said he feared that all of Ithaca would be after Odysseus for what he had done to the suitors. However, they went to the house where Telemachus had arranged a meal. Laertes bathed and dressed and Athena enhanced his appearance before he sat down to eat.

In the town the news of the death of the suitors spread. The dead were buried and a meeting was addressed by Eupithes, who named Odysseus a criminal. He had returned without his ships, he said, without his crew and set upon the suitors. Justice was demanded. As the people were stirred to anger against their king, the minstrel and Medon addressed the crowd. They told how they had seen one of the divine gods, disguised as Mentor, urging on and helping Odysseus. At these words, a certain Halitherses spoke. It was their own fault, he said. They had done nothing when their sons plundered the estate of Odysseus and insulted his wife. But the Eupeithes and the people would not listen and took up their arms.

Odysseus, Telemachus and Laertes had finished eating when they saw the army of men approach. Athena, disguised as Mentor, joined the three, telling Laertes to throw his spear. The weapon struck Eupeithes and Odysseus and Telemachus took up their weapons and attacked the front line. Athena stopped the fighting with a great cry and in terror the Ithacans

fled. Odysseus prepared to give chase but Zeus aimed a thunderbolt which landed in front of Athena who commanded Odysseus to stay his hand. And in the guise of Mentor, Athena brought peace to the people of Ithaca.

And so Homer brought the Odyssey to an end. There is a

Hermes speaks
to the spirits
of the dead

story told that the families of the suitors brought a case against Odysseus and he was exiled for ten years. Perhaps this is when he took up his oar as instructed by the seer, Teiresias, and wandered until he found a people who did not know the sea, buried his oar and sacrificed to Poseidon as instructed.

There are tales that the patient Penelope did not remain faithful to him and that she was sent away, to her father in Sparta. She stayed in Mantineia on her way home and by Hermes had a son, the god Pan, shepherd deity of Arcadia.

Some say that Odysseus died of old age, but another tale tells of a son by Circe, Telegonus, who set out in search of him. When the young man and his crew landed at Ithaca, the ageing Odysseus helped Telemachus defend the island against the newcomers and Odysseus was killed by a spear thrown by Telegonus.

Part 4

Crumbs from The Poet's Table

Artists, sculptors, poets and dramatists down the ages have been inspired by The Poet. **Aeschylus**, who lived from 525 - 456 BC, was a Greek dramatist and founder of Greek tragedy. His great trilogy, the Oresteia, owes much to Homer's Odyssey. It was Aeschylus who said,

"We are all eating crumbs from the great table of Homer."

Homer's Achilles was the hero of **Alexander the Great**, 356 - 323 BC. He is said to have kept a copy of the Iliad under his pillow and many of his actions during his long campaigns were influenced by Homer's Achilles.

Virgil, 70 - 19 BC was inspired by Homer to write the Aenid, taking themes from both the Iliad and the Odyssey. Aeneas was the son of Aphrodite and Anchises, according to Homer. He fought in the Trojan war and Virgil, in the Aenid, described Aeneas' escape from Troy and his seven year wanderings in the Mediterranean before he finally reached Latium and founded Rome.

In the fifteenth century AD, the works of Homer were published in Florence and came to the notice of European philosophers. But until **George Chapman** 1599 - 1634 AD, translated Homer into English, Homer was a poet heard of, admired but not really known by ordinary people, for the language his work was written in was archaic and difficult.

Chapman was a poet and dramatist whose translation of the Iliad inspired **William Shakespeare**, 1564 - 1634, to write the play Troilus and Cressida. The work is based on the killing of Priam's son, Hector, by Achilles.

Between 1720 and 1725 AD, **Alexander Pope**, poet and satirist, translated Homer into rhyming couplets. The gods and

her s were given the Latin equivalent of their names. But it
wa: Chapman's translation that inspired the poet, **John Keats**,
17(- 1821, to write:-

> *"Much have I travell'd in the realms of gold,*
> *And many goodly states and kingdoms seen:*
> *Round many western islands have I been*
> *Which bards in fealty to Apollo hold.*
> *Oft of one wide expanse had I been told*
> *That deep brow'd Homer ruled as his desmesne:*
> *Yet did I never breathe its pure serene*
> *Till I heard Chapman speak out loud and bold:*
> *Then felt I like some watcher of the skies*
> *When a new planet swims into his ken;*
> *Or like stout Cortez when with eagle eyes*
> *He star'd at the Pacific - and all his men*
> *Look'd at each other with a wild surmise -*
> *Silent, upon a peak in Darien."*

The English sculptor, **John Flaxman**, 1755 - 1828, was
inspired by the description in the Iliad to cast the Shield of
Achilles, in silver gilt. The original was said by Homer to have
been cast by the smith god, Hephaestus. Flaxman also
illustrated Alexander Pope's translation of the Iliad and his
friend, **William Blake**, later re-engraved some of the drawings.
A painting by the French artist, **Ingres**, executed circa 1801,
illustrates a scene from the Iliad and in 1827 the artist painted
"The Apotheosis of Homer", a painting, now in the Paris
Louvre, which depicts the crowning of Homer as a god.
The American poet **Walt Whitman**, 1819 - 1892, is said to
have ridden on top of an open bus, hair flying in the wind,
reciting Homer aloud.

Nearer to our own time, during the First World War, the poet **Rupert Brooke** was on his way to Gallipoli in 1915. Gallipoli was not far from Troy and although Brooke died before reaching the battleground, news of the terrible fighting must have reached him and he had the Iliad in mind when he wrote the following lines while on his journey:

"They say Achilles in the darkness stirred
And Priam and his fifty sons
Wake all amazed, and hear the guns
And shake for Troy again".

THE END

Index

A

Achaeans, 11, 23, 26, 29, 37, 41, 43, 49, 156

Achilles, 18, 19, 21, 23, 24, 25, 27, 28, 33, 40, 41, 46, 47, 48, 49, 51, 54, 55, 65, 67, 68, 69, 70, 71, 72, 73, 74, 75, 76, 77, 78, 80, 81, 82, 83, 84, 85, 86, 87, 88, 89, 90, 91, 92, 93, 94, 95, 96, 97, 106, 109, 121, 133, 168, 173, 174, 175

Aegisthus, 100, 107, 111, 133

Aegyptius, 103

Aeneas, 36, 61, 73, 74, 81, 82, 173

Aeneias, 35, 36

Aenid, 173

Aeolus, 128

Aeschylus, 173

Agamemmnon, 18

Agamemnon, 18, 19, 21, 23, 24, 25, 26, 27, 28, 30, 31, 32, 34, 37, 41, 43, 44, 45, 47, 48, 49, 50, 52, 53, 55, 62, 63, 64, 68, 78, 80, 89, 90, 93, 97, 100, 106, 107, 108, 111, 133, 142, 168

Agelaus, 161

Agenor, 85

Ajax, 28, 31, 33, 42, 44, 46, 47, 49, 50, 54, 57, 59, 60, 61, 64, 67, 68, 72, 73, 74, 92, 97, 106, 111, 133

Alcathous, 61

Alcimedon, 69, 74

Alcinous, 115, 118, 119, 120, 121, 122, 123, 133, 137, 138

Alcmene, 133

Alexander Pope, 173, 174

Alexander the Great, 17, 173

Amphinomus, 148, 152, 160

Andromache, 40, 88, 97

Anteia, 38

Antenor, 43, 53

Anticleia, 131

Antilochus, 74, 75, 90, 91, 92, 97

Antinous, 30, 103, 105, 112, 148, 151, 152, 162, 163, 164

Aphrodite, 29, 31, 32, 35, 36, 37, 62, 81, 85, 121, 122, 173

Apollo, 14, 23, 24, 25, 32, 36, 41, 52, 65, 66, 70, 71, 72, 73, 74, 81, 83, 85, 86, 90, 94, 96, 97, 121, 122, 131, 135, 136, 163, 174

Apollodorus, 98

Ares, 33, 34, 36, 39, 65, 67, 81, 85, 121, 122

Arete, 117, 118, 133